BIBS

DAILY DEVOTIONAL

A **30-week** daily Bible study through **Proverbs**

(Name)_____

Book Contents

Cycles

BIBS
BIG IDEA BIBLE STUDY

BIBS is a suite of devotionals taking the student through many books of the Bible. While each devotional includes its own directions on what to fill out each day, the instructional book (pictured left) was designed to be the in-depth description of each step.

BIBS: Big Idea Bible Study (not to be confused with this *BIBS Devotional*) answers the three main questions of Bible study and provides a format on which to build. The three questions are WHY do we study the Bible, HOW should we study it, and WHAT should we do with it?

The *BIBS* devotionals are all-inclusive and self explanatory, but the book *BIBS: Big Idea Bible Study* provides a richer explanation of the BIBS process.

For more information on ordering, please contact Calvary Baptist Church at (951) 676-8700, or find them on Amazon.com.

The BIBS Devotional Book is a daily Bible reading and study plan. It is designed to guide the reader in both an in-depth study of a certain short passage every day, as well as weekly overview readings of the surrounding chapters to provide context.

Ryan Rench is the youth pastor at **Calvary Baptist Church** in Temecula, CA, Pastor W. M. Rench. He has been on staff since May, 2010, and was trained at Heartland Baptist Bible College in Oklahoma City, OK (BA, MM). He also interned under Pastor Wayne Hardy of Bible Baptist Church in Stillwater, OK.

Note from the author: "There are two main reasons I do not often use or recommend most devotional books or most things written for teens. First, they cater to this false idea that teens are somehow less intelligent and need things 'dumbed down' for them to get it. Wrong! Those in their teen years are highly motivated to excel at whatever they're challenged to do. BIBS simply challenges them to know their Bibles if they're up to it.

"Second, most devotionals have the reader read very little of the Bible and think very little for himself. Then, if there is a biblical text to read--and sometimes it is only one verse(!)--the devotional tells the reader what to think about that text. God's Word IS saying something in every text, but discovering it for myself and applying it to myself is much more lasting. Following the BIBS format offers both the depths of Scripture AND the flow of thought of the context of Scripture. It is a guide to help you hear from God and a tool to help you understand and apply His desires for your life."

B.I.B.S. Created in 2012. All quotations use the King James Bible.

PREFACE TO THIS EDITION

What started as a series of Wednesday night Bible study lessons has since blossomed to this book (as well as the whole suite of books). The Teens of Faith (the youth group of our church) benefited spiritually as they worked through this devotional day by day. Those who completed the devotional were able to attend our first missions trip to Alaska, and the weekly Wednesday night check-ins were refreshing and challenging (hence the Thursday-to-Wednesday layout).

The book of Proverbs is full of riches, and is specifically written to young people. At its heart is a call to fear God. God's wisdom is provided only in a fearful, earnest search for it. Wise people do not just fall into wisdom; they search it out, as if searching for hidden treasure. Beginning in 2015, the Teens of Faith Sunday school class has been studying the book of Proverbs. The theme question of the series is "What is the wise thing to do?"

Since Bible preaching is crucial to any Christian's spiritual walk, our teens benefit by using their personal devotions as a means to further drive home what they receive through weekly preaching. Although you might not hear these texts explained through preaching, we pray they sink in as you perform your own study using the BIBS process.

The Bible is all that will matter...

Before getting into the BIBS book you have to first know that the Bible is the only thing that will matter to you in 246 years (random...). Or 1,000 years. It's the only thing that will protect you from the nasty messes in life. Seems crazy NOT to read it!

Personal discipline

Are you willing to develop the discipline of Bible study without someone forcing this on you? If so, this Bible study will be the best thing you do over the next few weeks. If not, this whole Bible study will be unneeded.

You'll commit to band, martial arts, sports practice or even school... but will you commit to stretch yourself spiritually? This Bible study will outlast ALL those other things in your life, so really take it seriously. At LEAST commit to <u>four full weeks</u>. That's only two cycles through the format we're using, and it could take as little as 15 minutes per day.

Commit now?

Maybe you will commit to the full devotional. Maybe you just want to commit to the first section. Will you commit right now?

1. Commit to only 2 cycles

Lord, with your help, I want to commit to at least two cycles (4 weeks) of this Bible study devotional.

*(Print Name)*_____

*(Signature)*_____

When and where?

If you made that commitment, write the time and location you'll do your devotions every day:

*(Time)*_____

*(Location)*_____

2. Full commitment of my mind

Now, if you're willing to commit to work through the whole BIBS book, to <u>honestly work and think</u> and not just "get by," then sign your name below.

Notice, you're not committing to filling out

every line or getting every answer right. Nor are you committing to daily work (because then if you miss one day you feel like you've failed God!). You're committing to be honest before God and sincerely asking Him to make this Bible study devotional something that will help you.

God, before You and only with Your help, I commit to <u>honestly work</u> to make this something valuable to my spiritual life.

(Signature)_____

(Date)_____

That's it! This is between you and God now! Always remember, "...a just *man* falleth seven times, and riseth up again." (Proverbs 24:16) You'll probably miss a day or two here and there, but DON'T let that get you out of the habit once you've built it. **It may take about three weeks to get into the habit** of doing devotions if you're not in the habit already.

Stick it out, and by the fourth week it will be much easier. If it's *real*, over time you won't be able to put your Bible *down*. That's a much better problem than never picking it up!

Why call it Big Idea Bible Study?

A thank-you card has a specific intent: thanking someone for something.

A letter of recommendation has a specific intent: recommending someone or something.

A love letter has a specific and single intent: wishing someone a happy birthday. (Wait... what?! No.)

When you sit to write any kind of note or draft some sort of business letter, there is almost always a specific and single reason. Letters and notes often basically say only one thing: "Thank you," "I recommend...," or "I love you." for example. The body of the letter has

lots to say, but the whole letter basically only says one thing.

Deep and wide

Bible study is both deep and wide. Sometimes people get lost in the "depths" of Scripture and at other times they breeze so quickly through the chapters that they miss the gold nuggets along the way.

To me, the best times in my life are when I am deep in God's Word.

However, I cannot truly get deeper into a biblical text until I've read several chapters before and after it and got into the biblical author's flow of thought.

Bible study needs both—both the depths of the text AND the full context (or flow) of the biblical author's thoughts.

So?

The Big Idea Bible Study is designed to be both an **in-depth** look at certain portions of Scripture as well as a **birds-eye view** of the biblical text. Further, with BIBS we desire to analyze certain portions of Scripture to see:

1) What the original intent was
2) What the timeless truth is
3) What it means for us today

ROCKS
It is easier to catch a rock than a handful of sand. The Bible is not full of a bunch of unrelated thoughts (sand). It is full of ideas... rocks!

Say! What's the BIG IDEA?

3 STEPS
TO VIEW EVERY TEXT

Taken from Howard Hendricks' *Living By the Book*, each Bible text needs to be viewed three ways: OBSERVATION, INTERPRETATION, and APPLICATION. Bookmark or dog-ear these pages to refer back to them for the first few weeks. They'll help you when you're stuck for what to look for in your study.

OBSERVATION
THE BIRDS-EYE VIEW

INTERPRETATION
WHAT IS GOD SAYING?

APPLICATION
WHAT IS GOD SAYING TO ME?

OBSERVATION

The birds-eye view

The first view, OBSERVATION, is the broad overview of what's going on in the text. It's as if you're flying way up in the sky and surveying the whole land (although I doubt this fat little bird can fly!). Ask broad questions:

- Why was the book written in the first place?
- What happened in this story before this text?
- To whom is it written?
- What's the problem with mankind that God is trying to fix with this text? (It HAS to address some need... what is it?)
- What *type* of writing is it?
    o Narrative – A broad, often long story with a lesson or moral.
    o Law – God's commandments for His people Israel.
    o Prophets – Warnings from God to His people Israel.
    o Psalms – Songs and prayers to or about God.
    o Wisdom – Proverbs and poetry.
    o Gospels – The story of Christ from different perspectives.
    o Acts – A history of the church in transition.
    o Parable – A story with a single point.
    o Epistle – A letter to a church or individual.
    o Prophecy – Foretelling of judgments and hope.
    o For more information on genres, see **Appendix 2.**

INTERPRETATION

What is God saying?

The second view, INTERPRETATION, answers the basic question, "What is God saying?" If God said things that meant something to them (the original readers), what was He saying? In the Bible characters' terms, what was God fixing or teaching or encouraging or commanding *them* to do? If we know what God *said,* we can know what God is *saying.* You've already got a good start through OBSERVATION, but now let's go deeper by learning INTERPRETATION.

Read

Your best tool will be reading. Read through the text (the small "chunk" of Scripture) and try to get a broad idea of what it's saying.

Reread

Now, go back and read those few verses again. Think harder this time. Try to get an overall idea of what's going on.

Flag Words

You'll come across words you don't understand, key words or repeating words through your reading. Either mark them and come back, or get your tools out and look them up as you go. The King James is not difficult to understand... you just need a couple tools to help along the way.

"WHAT AM I TALKING ABOUT?"

You're trying to answer the question, "What am I talking about?" What's this text about overall? Don't get lost in all the little details... think BIG idea.

If the BIG IDEA is like a tree, then lets just start with the main part--the trunk. This is the trunk. "What am I talking about?" Start broadly:

Word

You've read and reread. You've looked up confusing words and noticed repeating words. Now **what one word comes to mind as an overall thought** for this text? (Please see Appendix 3 for examples.)

Phrase

Now, suppose that one word is *Praise*. **Narrow that down** a little. Is this text saying everything about praise? No. Whose praise? Who is praising? What about praise? What kind? There are a lot of directions this could go!

Suppose (as you see from our example in Appendix 3) our phrase then becomes *Praise of God*. That narrows it down, but it's still not enough. We all know a lot about praising God. What about it?! Go further...

Sentence

Now, **expand that phrase into a sentence.** What about praising God? Who should? Don't come up with the sentence on your own. Base it on the text.

If you could boil this text down into a sentence, *what is this text talking about?*

Suppose, again from our example, that the sentence is "We should praise the Lord." That's a full sentence -- a complete thought. It is definite. It is concise. It is a rock.

Summary

In summary, the way to answer the question "What am I talking about?" is to follow this progression:

- **Read**
- **Reread**
- **Flag Words**
- **Boil Down to a Word**
- **Expand to a Phrase**
- **Summarize in a Sentence**

Tools of the trade

Some good tools for observation and interpretation are a simple Bible reference tool for your computer, a Bible dictionary and/or a study Bible. Free Bible software can be downloaded at www.e-sword.net. Or, several online sources such as classic.net.bible.org will have Strongs reference numbers under the King James tab. Good dictionaries such as Webster's 1828 can be downloaded for free through E-Sword. Further, a good study Bible will give you an overview of the book before you begin reading; and it will give you helpful insights such as cross references, maps and further explanations as you are reading through a text.

Warning: use man's wisdom sparingly! Your goal is to hear from God directly, so don't rely on these Bible study tools as a crutch to "get the right answer." You're not after the "right answer." You are after hearing from God, so spend most of your time in His Word!

"WHAT AM I SAYING ABOUT WHAT I'M TALKING ABOUT?"

If the BIG IDEA is a tree and we've already found the trunk, lets fill in all the branches -- all the little details that describe or enhance the trunk. These "branches" are all the details that say stuff about what we're talking about.

Question word

If you could turn your sentence into a question, what **question word** would you use? Is this a **who, what, where, when, why** or **how** text?

Question

OK, once you've found your word, **turn your sentence into a question.** For our running example, our sentence was:

"We should praise the Lord."

If our question word is *why,* then our question now is:

"**Why** should we praise the Lord?"

Answer(s)

Once you have the basic question, simply **answer it from the text.** These answers will fill out your tree with all the leaves and branches.

Why should we praise the Lord? Well, there are two answers, or two branches:

* Because his merciful kindness is great toward us.
* Because the truth of the Lord endureth forever.

BIBS INTERPRETATION STEPS

Wondering what God is talking about in His Word? Follow these steps and you should have a pretty good idea

* **Read**
* **Reread**
* **Flag Words**
* **Boil Down to a Word**
* **Expand to a Phrase**
* **Summarize in a Sentence**
* **Rephrase into a Question**
* **Answer the Question**
* **Combine into a Sentence**

APPLICATION

What is God saying *to me*?

There's only one *interpretation* to each passage--there's only one right answer to what God *said*. BUT... when it comes to APPLICATION (what God is *saying* to me) there are tons of ways this could go!

Overall, what did you learn?

God speaks in SO many different ways through His Word, and maybe He spoke to you from one little phrase, the whole "Big Idea," or even just in one word you studied. God is always speaking through His Word, so how did He speak to you through this text? How does it apply to you? What did you learn from it? How has it helped? How has it encouraged you? What did it challenge you to do?

Application days

Here's where we get to the hard part. It's easy to learn stuff about God. It's easy to know you're supposed to watch your mouth, guard your mind, be in church, give the gospel, care for others, obey your parents...

Those Bible truths are easy to know, but HARD to live. Every "Application Day" will need to be a serious time between you and God. First, pray and ask Him to reveal hidden sin. Next, ask Him to help you overcome it. Finally, ask Him if there's even anything small in your life that could be changed. He will reveal "big" and "small" sins in your life, and it is your job to change them through His power.

"Application Days" come around a couple times per week in the BIBS format. While you will be learning and growing **every day**, the "Application Day" should especially be a clear-minded, open-hearted soul searching time before God.

Self deception

*But be ye doers of the word and not hearers only, **deceiving your own selves.** James 1:22*

According to James 1:22, the more you hear the Word and don't do anything about it, the more self-deceived you become. That's scary... you don't even know *right now* if you're deceived (otherwise you wouldn't be deceived!).

DO something!

Determine to not ONLY know stuff about the Bible but to actually do stuff with your knowledge. If the "Big Idea" you find is something like, "Paul's desire to see the Thessalonians walk worthy drove him to self sacrifice," you can respond a couple different ways:

"That's nice. Paul sacrificed for others. What a swell guy. Time for me to go to school!"

Or...

*"Wow. Paul was so passionate about helping others, he sacrificed a lot. How have I **sacrificed** lately? I really haven't. Maybe I should.*

"What can I sacrifice?! I'm only a teen! What do I have to give in self-sacrifice?

*"Well, I guess I DO have a little **money**. It's not much, but I know I need to sacrifice something, so I'm going to start giving to missions every week by faith.*

*"I don't have much, but I DO have some spare **time**. I waste a lot on video games. I doubt Paul did that. I need to spend my time better. I'm going to limit my video games to 1 hour and spend the rest of the time on my devotions (or exercise, or writing notes, or...)*

*"I don't have much experience, but I CAN **work**. I want to donate my youth and my energy to help out wherever I can. Not for payment but to simply serve. I'll call the church today to see where I can work."*

Make a plan

Once you've decided to do something, write out your plan. **Be specific.**

So that I am not deceived, I plan to:

"Sacrifice by committing to $2/week.

"Time my video games and stop at one hour total. I'll spend the spare time doing my chores, reading _____, writing encouraging notes to _____, and exercising for ____ minutes per day.

"I'm going to call my youth pastor and set up a time to do yard work around the church. I'll also ask him this week at church if there's anything I can do throughout the week."

Specifically, what is one thing you can do this week that will be acting on what you've learned from God's Word?

Conclude in prayer

God's been speaking and you've been responding by promising to act on His Word. Now conclude in prayer and ask God's help and strength as you do what you committed to do. (Dan. 1:8)

HOW TO
USE THIS BOOK

 IN CYCLES

A cycle is a two-week study of a large portion of Scripture (usually two or three chapters.) In each cycle you will read the whole portion several times, sometimes for several days in a row. (You'll see more details in the daily breakdown.)

The cycle is designed to give you the broad overview of the whole context, and to help you get into the author's flow of thought.

If you signed the first commitment at the beginning of the book, you decided that you wanted to commit to two cycles. The first cycle you will read the same two or three chapters almost every day (e.g. 1 Thessalonians 1-3), and the second cycle you will read the next couple of chapters (e.g. 1 Thessalonians 4-5) almost every day.

WEEKLY

Each week starts on Thursday and will involve all three steps of the BIBS format:

- Observation
- Interpretation
- Application

Each day is a different view of Scripture, and most days will overlap with each other. Reviewing weekly helps keep the big picture in mind.

Each week will keep in focus the larger portion of Scripture found in the cycle, but it will also break the cycle down into smaller passages. The first week takes it slowly and discovers the background of the text, and the second week moves quicker because you are already familiar with the background.

DAILY

Daily reading and writing are what the BIBS format is all about. Each day will be a different assignment than the day before, although each day will also repeat a lot of information from the whole week.

Some days will be a lot of reading, some will be writing, and some will be thinking. Don't try to do every step in one day. The BIBS format is spread over a week for a reason. You'll have plenty of time to get to each part.

However, if you do work ahead... that's okay too!

Daily Checklist

The following list is the basic idea for how each day will look. Certain days will have lined sections to write on, and other days will be very simple and short. Cycle 2 Week 2 will only have one Application Day and no Observation Day and certain other weeks may vary. Each step is explained further each day.

 THURSDAY Reading Day (Observation)

1. Pray
2. Study Bible – read intro paragraph
3. Read whole book (or large portion)
4. Note text 1 & 2

 FRIDAY Rereading Day

1. Read 2 chapters
2. Reread text 1
3. One word
4. Phrase

 SATURDAY Thinking Day (Interpretation)

1. Read 2 chapters
2. Reread text 1
3. Review yesterday's phrase
4. Expand to a sentence (tree trunk)
5. Turn it into a question (what question word?)
6. Answer the question (branches)

 SUNDAY Application Day (Application)

1. Read full chapter
2. Combine "Trunk" and "Branches"
3. What is God saying? (BIG IDEA - full tree)
4. What is God saying TO ME? Application.
5. Write plan

 MONDAY Rereading Day

1. Read 2 chapters
2. Reread text 2
3. One word
4. Phrase

 TUESDAY Thinking Day (Interpretation)

1. Read 2 chapters
2. Reread text 2
3. Review yesterday's phrase
4. Expand to a sentence (tree trunk)
5. Turn it into a question (what question word?)
6. Answer the question (branches)

 WEDNESDAY Application Day (Application)

7. Read full chapter Combine "Trunk" and "Branches"
8. What is God saying? (BIG IDEA - full tree)
9. What is God saying TO ME? Application.
10. Write plan
11. Discuss texts 1 & 2 in church

Ready to get going? *God, please help us as we learn your will through your Word.*

CYCLE 1

Proverbs 1-2

WEEK 1

*Initial each daily step when done.

 ## DAY 1 - THURSDAY
Reading Day (Observation)

___ **1. Pray.** Open in prayer. Ask God's forgiveness for known sin and ask for His help in today's study.

___ **2. Background.** (see p.8 or Appendix 3 for more ideas)

_____

_____

___ **3. Read Proverbs.** Read Prov. 1-5 (or more) to get the overall concept.

4. Note the text divisions. See what's coming up this week. Write the two texts you'll be studying below:

_____

 ## DAY 2 - FRIDAY
Rereading Day

___ **1. Pray.**

___ **2. Read.** Read Prov. 1-2.

___ **3. Reread text.** Read Prov. 1:1-6.

4. Word. What word generally describes this text?

_____

5. Phrase. Now what about that word? Expand it to a phrase:

_____

Note: if you want to expand it to a sentence, go ahead!

DAY 3 - SATURDAY
Thinking Day (Interpretation)

___ **1. Pray.**

___ **2. Read.** Read Prov. 1-2.

___ **3. Reread text.** Read Prov. 1:1-6.

4. Review. Write the phrase you ended up with yesterday:

_____

5. Sentence. Now expand that phrase to a sentence:

_____

6. Question. If that sentence could be turned into a question, circle the word that could be used (who, what, where, when, why, how).

Now rewrite the sentence in the form of a question:

_____

7. Answer(s). Write the many answers to your question below. These answers are all the ideas taken from the text.

_____

_____

_____

_____

_____

DAY 4 - SUNDAY
Application Day (Application)

___ **1. Pray.**

___ **2. Read.** Read Prov. 1.

3. Combine. Try to combine the "Trunk" and the "Branches" into a complete thought here:

_____

_____

4. Apply. The BIG IDEA you just wrote is what God said. And that's what He's still saying. So now... what is He saying <u>to you</u>?

First, write some general things you learned.

_____

_____

_____

_____

Next, whether you learned it from one word, the big idea, or even some random, obscure thought you had, write any other application you can think of:

_____

_____

5. Plan. Write your plan to DO something different in your life because of what you have learned.

So that I am not deceived, I plan to:

_____

_____

_____

DAY 5 - MONDAY
Rereading Day

___ **1. Pray.**

___ **2. Read.** Read Prov. 1-2.

___ **3. Reread text.** Read Prov. 1:7-19.

4. Word. What word generally describes this text?

_____

5. Phrase. Now what about that word? Expand it to a phrase:

_____

Note: if you want to expand it to a sentence, go ahead!

DAY 6 - TUESDAY
Thinking Day (Interpretation)

___ **1. Pray.**

___ **2. Read.** Read Prov. 1-2.

___ **3. Reread text.** Read Prov. 1:7-19.

4. Review. Write the phrase you ended up with yesterday:

_____

5. Sentence. Now expand that phrase to a sentence:

_____

6. Question. If that sentence could be turned into a question, circle the word that could be used (who, what, where, when, why, how).

Now rewrite the sentence in the form of a question:

_____

7. Answer(s). Write the many answers to your question below. These answers are all the ideas taken from the text.

_____

_____

_____

_____

_____

_____

DAY 7 - WEDNESDAY
Application Day (Application)

___ **1. Pray.**

___ **2. Read.** Read Prov. 1.

3. Combine. Try to combine the "Trunk" and the "Branches" into a complete thought here:

_____

_____

4. Apply. The BIG IDEA you just wrote is what God said. And that's what He's still saying. So now... what is He saying <u>to you</u>?

First, write some general things you learned.

_____

_____

_____

_____

_____

_____

Next, whether you learned it from one word, the big idea, or even some random, obscure thought you had, write any other application you can think of:

_____

_____

5. Plan. Write your plan to DO something different in your life because of what you have learned.

So that I am not deceived, I plan to:

_____

_____

_____

_____

WEEK 2

*Initial each daily step when done.

DAY 1 - THURSDAY
Rereading Day (much OBS. has been done)

___ **1. Pray.**

___ **2. Read.** Read Prov. 1-3.

___ **3. Reread text.** Read Prov. 1:20-33.

4. Word. What word generally describes this text?

_____

5. Phrase. Now what about that word? Expand it to a phrase:

_____

6. Sentence. Expand that phrase to a sentence:

_____

DAY 2 - FRIDAY
Thinking Day (Interpretation)

___ **1. Pray.**

___ **2. Read.** Read Prov. 1-2.

___ **3. Reread text.** Read Prov. 1:20-33.

4. Review. Write the sentence you ended up with yesterday:

_____

5. Question. If that sentence could be turned into a question, circle the word that could be used (who, what, where, when, why, how).

Now rewrite the sentence in the form of a question:

_____

6. Answer(s). Write the many answers to your question below. These answers are all the ideas taken from the text.

_____

_____

_____

_____

_____

_____

7. Apply. Tomorrow will not be application, so write a few thoughts of your own below:

_____

_____

_____

_____

DAY 3 - SATURDAY
Rereading Day (Interpretation)

___ **1. Pray.**

___ **2. Read.** Read Prov. 2-3.

___ **3. Reread text.** Read Prov. 2:1-9.

4. Word. What word generally describes this text?

_____

5. Phrase. Now what about that word? Expand it to a phrase:

_____

6. Sentence. Expand that phrase to a sentence:

_____

DAY 4 - SUNDAY
Thinking Day (Interpretation)

___ **1. Pray.**

___ **2. Read.** Read Prov. 1-2.

___ **3. Reread text.** Read Prov. 2:1-9.

4. Review. Write the sentence you ended up with yesterday:

_____

5. Question. If that sentence could be turned into a question, circle the word that could be used (who, what, where, when, why, how).

Now rewrite the sentence in the form of a question:

_____

6. Answer(s). Write the many answers to your question below. These answers are all the ideas taken from the text.

_____

_____

_____

_____

7. Apply. Tomorrow will not be application, so write a few thoughts of your own below:

_____

_____

DAY 5 - MONDAY
Rereading Day (Interpretation)

___ **1. Pray.**

___ **2. Read.** Read Prov. 1-2.

___ **3. Reread text.** Read Prov. 2:10-22

4. Word. What word generally describes this text?

_____

5. Phrase. Now what about that word? Expand it to a phrase:

_____

6. Sentence. Expand that phrase to a sentence:

_____

DAY 6 - TUESDAY
Thinking Day (Interpretation)

___ **1. Pray.**

___ **2. Read.** Read Prov. 1-2.

___ **3. Reread text.** Read Prov. 2:10-22.

4. Review. Write the sentence you ended up with yesterday:

_____

5. Question. If that sentence could be turned into a question, circle the word that could be used (who, what, where, when, why, how).

Now rewrite the sentence in the form of a question:

_____

6. Answer(s). Write the many answers to your question below. These answers are all the ideas taken from the text.

_____

_____

_____

_____

_____

_____

_____

DAY 7 - WEDNESDAY
Application Day (Application)

___ **1. Pray.**

___ **2. Read.** Read Prov. 2.

3. Combine. Write the three "trees" you found (from days 2, 4, 6):

_____

_____

_____

_____

4. Apply. The BIG IDEAS you just wrote were what God said. And that's what He's still saying. So now... what is He saying <u>to you</u>?

First, write some general things you learned.

_____

_____

_____

_____

_____

_____

Next, whether you learned it from one word, the big idea, or even some random, obscure thought you had, write any other application you can think of:

_____

_____

_____

_____

_____

_____

_____

_____

5. Plan. Write your plan to DO something different in your life because of what you have learned.

So that I am not deceived, I plan to:

_____

_____

_____

_____

_____

_____

6. Discuss. Find someone to discuss your Bible study with. Even if it's something small that you learned, it will be a blessing to others. Remember, you're not trying to get the "right answer." You're trying to hear from God and change into His image!

CYCLE 2
Proverbs 3-4

WEEK 1

*Initial each daily step when done.

DAY 1 - THURSDAY
Reading Day (Observation)

___ **1. Pray.** Open in prayer. Ask God's forgiveness for known sin and ask for His help in today's study.

___ **2. Background.** If you have a study tool (online source, study Bible, computer software, commentary...), read some background on the book. Write some things you learned here (see p.8 and Appendix 3 for some ideas.):

_____

_____

_____

_____

___ **3. Read Proverbs.** Read chapters 2-6 (or more) to get the overall concept.

4. Note the text divisions. See what's coming up this week. Write the two texts you'll be studying below:

_____

DAY 2 - FRIDAY
Rereading Day

___ **1. Pray.**

___ **2. Read.** Read Prov. 3-4.

___ **3. Reread text.** Read Prov. 3:1-10.

4. Word. What word generally describes this text?

_____

5. Phrase. Now what about that word? Expand it to a phrase:

_____

Note: if you want to expand it to a sentence, go ahead!

DAY 3 - SATURDAY
Thinking Day (Interpretation)

___ **1. Pray.**

___ **2. Read.** Read Prov. 3-4.

___ **3. Reread text.** Read Prov. 3:1-10.

4. Review. Write the phrase you ended up with yesterday:

_____

5. Sentence. Now expand that phrase to a sentence:

_____

6. Question. If that sentence could be turned into a question, circle the word that could be used (who, what, where, when, why, how).

Now rewrite the sentence in the form of a question:

_____

7. Answer(s). Write the many answers to your question below. These answers are all the ideas taken from the text.

_____

_____

_____

DAY 4 - SUNDAY
Application Day (Application)

___ **1. Pray.**

___ **2. Read.** Read Prov. 3.

3. Combine. Try to combine the "Trunk" and the "Branches" into a complete thought here:

_____

_____

4. Apply. The BIG IDEA you just wrote is what God said. And that's what He's still saying. So now... what is He saying <u>to you</u>?

First, write some general things you learned.

_____

_____

_____

_____

_____

Next, whether you learned it from one word, the big idea, or even some random, obscure thought you had, write any other application you can think of:

_____

_____

5. Plan. Write your plan to DO something different in your life because of what you have learned.

So that I am not deceived, I plan to:

_____

_____

_____

_____

DAY 5 - MONDAY
Rereading Day

___ **1. Pray.**

___ **2. Read.** Read Prov. 3-4.

___ **3. Reread text.** Read Prov. 3:11-12.

4. Word. What word generally describes this text?

_____

5. Phrase. Now what about that word? Expand it to a phrase:

_____

Note: if you want to expand it to a sentence, go ahead!

DAY 6 - TUESDAY
Thinking Day (Interpretation)

___ **1. Pray.**

___ **2. Read.** Read Prov. 3-4.

___ **3. Reread text.** Read Prov. 3:11-12.

4. Review. Write the phrase you ended up with yesterday:

_____

5. Sentence. Now expand that phrase to a sentence:

_____

6. Question. If that sentence could be turned into a question, circle the word that could be used (who, what, where, when, why, how).

Now rewrite the sentence in the form of a question:

_____

7. Answer(s). Write the many answers to your question below. These answers are all the ideas taken from the text.

_____

_____

_____

_____

_____

_____

_____

DAY 7 - WEDNESDAY
Application Day (Application)

___ **1. Pray.**

___ **2. Read.** Read Prov. 3.

3. Combine. Try to combine the "Trunk" and the "Branches" into a complete thought here:

_____

_____

4. Apply. The BIG IDEA you just wrote is what God said. And that's what He's still saying. So now... what is He saying <u>to you</u>?

First, write some general things you learned.

_____

_____

_____

_____

_____

Next, whether you learned it from one word, the big idea, or even some random, obscure thought you had, write any other application you can think of:

_____

_____

5. Plan. Write your plan to DO something different in your life because of what you have learned.

So that I am not deceived, I plan to:

_____

_____

_____

_____

WEEK 2

*Initial each daily step when done.

DAY 1 - THURSDAY
Reading Day (Observation)

___ **1. Pray.**

___ **2. Background.** Write anything new you've learned here:

_____

_____

___ **3. Read Proverbs.** Read chapters 2-6 (or more) to get the overall concept.

4. Note the text divisions. See what's coming up this week. Write the two texts you'll be studying below:

_____

DAY 2 - FRIDAY
Rereading Day

___ **1. Pray.**

___ **2. Read.** Read Prov. 4.

___ **3. Reread text.** Read Prov 4:1-13.

4. Word. What word generally describes this text?

_____

5. Phrase. Now what about that word? Expand it to a phrase:

_____

DAY 3 - SATURDAY
Thinking Day (Interpretation)

___ **1. Pray.**

___ **2. Read.** Read Prov. 3-4.

___ **3. Reread text.** Read Prov. 4:1-13.

4. Review. Write the phrase you ended up with yesterday:

_____

5. Sentence. Now expand that phrase to a sentence:

_____

6. Question. If that sentence could be turned into a question, circle the word that could be used (who, what, where, when, why, how).

Now rewrite the sentence in the form of a question:

_____

7. Answer(s). Write the many answers to your question below. These answers are all the ideas taken from the text.

_____

_____

_____

_____

_____

_____

_____

DAY 4 - SUNDAY
Application Day (Application)

___ **1. Pray.**

___ **2. Read.** Read Prov. 4.

3. Combine. Try to combine the "Trunk" and the "Branches" into a complete thought here:

_____

_____

4. Apply. The BIG IDEA you just wrote is what God said. And that's what He's still saying. So now... what is He saying <u>to you</u>?

First, write some general things you learned.

_____

_____

_____

_____

Next, whether you learned it from one word, the big idea, or even some random, obscure thought you had, write any other application you can think of:

_____

_____

5. Plan. Write your plan to DO something different in your life because of what you have learned.

So that I am not deceived, I plan to:

_____

_____

_____

DAY 5 - MONDAY
Rereading Day

___ **1. Pray.**

___ **2. Read.** Read Prov. 3-4.

___ **3. Reread text.** Read Prov. 4:23-27.

4. Word. What word generally describes this text?

_____

5. Phrase. Now what about that word? Expand it to a phrase:

_____

Note: if you want to expand it to a sentence, go ahead!

DAY 6 - TUESDAY
Thinking Day (Interpretation)

___ **1. Pray.**

___ **2. Read.** Read Prov. 4-5.

___ **3. Reread text.** Read Prov. 4:23-27.

4. Review. Write the phrase you ended up with yesterday:

_____

5. Sentence. Now expand that phrase to a sentence:

_____

6. Question. If that sentence could be turned into a question, circle the word that could be used (who, what, where, when, why, how).

Now rewrite the sentence in the form of a question:

_____

7. Answer(s). Write the many answers to your question below. These answers are all the ideas taken from the text.

_____

_____

DAY 7 - WEDNESDAY
Application Day (Application)

____ **1. Pray.**

____ **2. Read.** Read Prov. 4.

3. Combine. Try to combine the "Trunk" and the "Branches" into a complete thought here:

_____

_____

4. Apply. The BIG IDEA you just wrote is what God said. And that's what He's still saying. So now... what is He saying <u>to you</u>?

First, write some general things you learned.

_____

_____

_____

Next, whether you learned it from one word, the big idea, or even some random, obscure thought you had, write any other application you can think of:

_____

_____

5. Plan. Write your plan to DO something different in your life because of what you have learned.

So that I am not deceived, I plan to:

_____

_____

_____

CYCLE 3
Proverbs 5-6

WEEK 1

*Initial each daily step when done.

DAY 1 - THURSDAY
Reading Day (Observation)

___ **1. Pray.** Open in prayer. Ask God's forgiveness for known sin and ask for His help in today's study.

___ **2. Background.** (see p.8 or Appendix 3 for more ideas)

_____

_____

___ **3. Read Proverbs.** Read chapters 4-8 (or more) to get the overall concept.

4. Note the text divisions. See what's coming up this week. Write the two texts you'll be studying below:

_____

DAY 2 - FRIDAY
Rereading Day

___ **1. Pray.**

___ **2. Read.** Read Prov. 5-6.

___ **3. Reread text.** Read Prov. 5:1-23.

4. Word. What word generally describes this text?

_____

5. Phrase. Now what about that word? Expand it to a phrase:

_____

Note: if you want to expand it to a sentence, go ahead!

DAY 3 - SATURDAY
Thinking Day (Interpretation)

___ **1. Pray.**

___ **2. Read.** Read Prov. 5-6.

___ **3. Reread text.** Read 5:1-23.

4. Review. Write the phrase you ended up with yesterday:

_____

5. Sentence. Now expand that phrase to a sentence:

_____

6. Question. If that sentence could be turned into a question, circle the word that could be used (who, what, where, when, why, how).

Now rewrite the sentence in the form of a question:

_____

7. Answer(s). Write the many answers to your question below. These answers are all the ideas taken from the text.

_____

_____

DAY 4 - SUNDAY
Application Day (Application)

___ **1. Pray.**

___ **2. Read.** Read Prov. 5.

3. Combine. Try to combine the "Trunk" and the "Branches" into a complete thought here:

_____

4. Apply. The BIG IDEA you just wrote is what God said. And that's what He's still saying. So now... what is He saying <u>to you</u>?

First, write some general things you learned.

_____

_____

_____

Next, whether you learned it from one word, the big idea, or even some random, obscure thought you had, write any other application you can think of:

_____

_____

5. Plan. Write your plan to DO something different in your life because of what you have learned.

So that I am not deceived, I plan to:

_____

_____

DAY 5 - MONDAY
Rereading Day

___ **1. Pray.**

___ **2. Read.** Read Prov. 5-6.

___ **3. Reread text.** Read Prov. 6:6-11.

4. Word. What word generally describes this text?

_____

5. Phrase. Now what about that word? Expand it to a phrase:

_____

Note: if you want to expand it to a sentence, go ahead!

DAY 6 - TUESDAY
Thinking Day (Interpretation)

___ **1. Pray.**

___ **2. Read.** Read Prov. 5-6.

___ **3. Reread text.** Read Prov. 6:6-11.

4. Review. Write the phrase you ended up with yesterday:

_____

5. Sentence. Now expand that phrase to a sentence:

_____

6. Question. If that sentence could be turned into a question, circle the word that could be used (who, what, where, when, why, how).

Now rewrite the sentence in the form of a question:

_____

7. Answer(s). Write the many answers to your question below. These answers are all the ideas taken from the text.

_____

_____

_____

DAY 7 - WEDNESDAY
Application Day (Application)

___ **1. Pray.**

___ **2. Read.** Read Prov. 6.

3. Combine. Try to combine the "Trunk" and the "Branches" into a complete thought here:

_____

_____

4. Apply. The BIG IDEA you just wrote is what God said. And that's what He's still saying. So now… what is He saying <u>to you</u>?

First, write some general things you learned.

_____

_____

Next, whether you learned it from one word, the big idea, or even some random, obscure thought you had, write any other application you can think of:

_____

_____

5. Plan. Write your plan to DO something different in your life because of what you have learned.

So that I am not deceived, I plan to:

_____

_____

_____

_____

WEEK 2

*Initial each daily step when done.

DAY 1 - THURSDAY
Rereading Day (much OBS. has been done)

___ **1. Pray.**

___ **2. Read.** Read Prov. 6-7.

___ **3. Reread text.** Read Prov. 6:12-15.

4. Word. What word generally describes this text?

_____

5. Phrase. Now what about that word? Expand it to a phrase:

_____

6. Sentence. Expand that phrase to a sentence:

_____

DAY 2 - FRIDAY
Thinking Day (Interpretation)

___ **1. Pray.**

___ **2. Read.** Read Prov. 5-6.

___ **3. Reread text.** Read Prov. 6:12-15.

4. Review. Write the sentence you ended up with yesterday:

_____

5. Question. If that sentence could be turned into a question, circle the word that could be used (who, what, where, when, why, how).

Now rewrite the sentence in the form of a question:

_____

6. Answer(s). Write the many answers to your question below. These answers are all the ideas taken from the text.

_____

_____

_____

7. Apply. Tomorrow will not be application, so write a few thoughts of your own below:

_____

_____

_____

DAY 3 - SATURDAY
Rereading Day (Interpretation)

___ **1. Pray.**

___ **2. Read.** Read Prov. 5-7.

___ **3. Reread text.** Read Prov. 6:16-19.

4. Word. What word generally describes this text?

_____

5. Phrase. Now what about that word? Expand it to a phrase:

_____

6. Sentence. Expand that phrase to a sentence:

_____

DAY 4 - SUNDAY
Thinking Day (Interpretation)

___ **1. Pray.**

___ **2. Read.** Read Prov. 5-6.

___ **3. Reread text.** Read Prov. 6:16-19.

4. Review. Write the sentence you ended up with yesterday:

_____

5. Question. If that sentence could be turned into a question, circle the word that could be used (who, what, where, when, why, how).

Now rewrite the sentence in the form of a question:

_____

6. Answer(s). Write the many answers to your question below. These answers are all the ideas taken from the text.

_____

_____

_____

_____

7. Apply. Tomorrow will not be application, so write a few thoughts of your own below:

_____

_____

DAY 5 - MONDAY
Rereading Day (Interpretation)

___ **1. Pray.**

___ **2. Read.** Read Prov. 5-6.

___ **3. Reread text.** Read Prov. 6:20-35

4. Word. What word generally describes this text?

_____

5. Phrase. Now what about that word? Expand it to a phrase:

_____

6. Sentence. Expand that phrase to a sentence:

_____

DAY 6 - TUESDAY
Thinking Day (Interpretation)

___ **1. Pray.**

___ **2. Read.** Read Prov. 5-6.

___ **3. Reread text.** Read Prov. 6:20-35.

4. Review. Write the sentence you ended up with yesterday:

_____

5. Question. If that sentence could be turned into a question, circle the word that could be used (who, what, where, when, why, how).

Now rewrite the sentence in the form of a question:

_____

6. Answer(s). Write the many answers to your question below. These answers are all the ideas taken from the text.

_____

_____

_____

_____

_____

DAY 7 - WEDNESDAY
Application Day (Application)

____ **1. Pray.**

____ **2. Read.** Read Prov. 6.

3. Combine. Write the three "trees" you found (from days 2, 4, 6):

_____

_____

_____

_____

4. Apply. The BIG IDEAS you just wrote were what God said. And that's what He's still saying. So now... what is He saying to you?

First, write some general things you learned.

_____

_____

_____

_____

_____

_____

Next, whether you learned it from one word, the big idea, or even some random, obscure thought you had, write any other application you can think of:

_____

_____

_____

_____

_____

_____

_____

_____

_____

_____

5. Plan. Write your plan to DO something different in your life because of what you have learned.

So that I am not deceived, I plan to:

_____

_____

_____

_____

_____

_____

_____

6. Discuss. Find someone to discuss your Bible study with. Even if it's something small that you learned, it will be a blessing to others. Remember, you're not trying to get the "right answer." You're trying to hear from God and change into His image!

CYCLE 4
Proverbs 7-8

WEEK 1

*Initial each daily step when done.

DAY 1 - THURSDAY
Reading Day (Observation)

___ **1. Pray.** Open in prayer. Ask God's forgiveness for known sin and ask for His help in today's study.

___ **2. Background.** If you have a study tool (online source, study Bible, computer software, commentary...), read some background on the book. Write some things you learned here (see p.8 and Appendix 3 for some ideas.):

_____

_____

_____

_____

___ **3. Read Proverbs.** Read chapters 6-10 (or more) to get the overall concept.

4. Note the text divisions. See what's coming up this week. Write the two texts you'll be studying below:

_____

DAY 2 - FRIDAY
Rereading Day

___ **1. Pray.**

___ **2. Read.** Read Prov. 7-8.

___ **3. Reread text.** Read Prov. 7:1-27.

4. Word. What word generally describes this text?

_____

5. Phrase. Now what about that word? Expand it to a phrase:

_____

Note: if you want to expand it to a sentence, go ahead!

DAY 3 - SATURDAY
Thinking Day (Interpretation)

___ **1. Pray.**

___ **2. Read.** Read Prov. 7-8.

___ **3. Reread text.** Read Prov. 7:1-27.

4. Review. Write the phrase you ended up with yesterday:

_____

5. Sentence. Now expand that phrase to a sentence:

_____

6. Question. If that sentence could be turned into a question, circle the word that could be used (who, what, where, when, why, how).

Now rewrite the sentence in the form of a question:

_____

7. Answer(s). Write the many answers to your question below. These answers are all the ideas taken from the text.

_____

_____

_____

_____

DAY 4 - SUNDAY
Application Day (Application)

___ **1. Pray.**

___ **2. Read.** Read Prov. 7.

3. Combine. Try to combine the "Trunk" and the "Branches" into a complete thought here:

_____

_____

4. Apply. The BIG IDEA you just wrote is what God said. And that's what He's still saying. So now... what is He saying <u>to you</u>?

First, write some general things you learned.

_____

_____

_____

_____

_____

Next, whether you learned it from one word, the big idea, or even some random, obscure thought you had, write any other application you can think of:

_____

_____

5. Plan. Write your plan to DO something different in your life because of what you have learned.

So that I am not deceived, I plan to:

_____

_____

_____

_____

DAY 5 - MONDAY
Rereading Day

___ **1. Pray.**

___ **2. Read.** Read Prov. 7-8.

___ **3. Reread text.** Read Prov. 8:1-11.

4. Word. What word generally describes this text?

5. Phrase. Now what about that word? Expand it to a phrase:

_____

Note: if you want to expand it to a sentence, go ahead!

DAY 6 - TUESDAY
Thinking Day (Interpretation)

___ **1. Pray.**

___ **2. Read.** Read Prov. 7-8.

___ **3. Reread text.** Read 8:1-11.

4. Review. Write the phrase you ended up with yesterday:

_____

5. Sentence. Now expand that phrase to a sentence:

_____

6. Question. If that sentence could be turned into a question, circle the word that could be used (who, what, where, when, why, how).

Now rewrite the sentence in the form of a question:

_____

7. Answer(s). Write the many answers to your question below. These answers are all the ideas taken from the text.

_____

_____

_____

_____

_____

_____

DAY 7 - WEDNESDAY
Application Day (Application)

___ **1. Pray.**

___ **2. Read.** Read Prov. 8.

3. Combine. Try to combine the "Trunk" and the "Branches" into a complete thought here:

_____

_____

4. Apply. The BIG IDEA you just wrote is what God said. And that's what He's still saying. So now... what is He saying <u>to you</u>?

First, write some general things you learned.

_____

_____

_____

_____

_____

_____

Next, whether you learned it from one word, the big idea, or even some random, obscure thought you had, write any other application you can think of:

_____

_____

5. Plan. Write your plan to DO something different in your life because of what you have learned.

So that I am not deceived, I plan to:

_____

_____

_____

_____

WEEK 2

*Initial each daily step when done.

DAY 1 - THURSDAY
Reading Day (Observation)

___ **1. Pray.**

___ **2. Background.** Write anything new you've learned here:

_____

_____

___ **3. Read Proverbs.** Read chapters 7-11 (or more) to get the overall concept.

4. Note the text divisions. See what's coming up this week. Write the two texts you'll be studying below:

_____

DAY 2 - FRIDAY
Rereading Day

___ **1. Pray.**

___ **2. Read.** Read Prov. 7-8.

___ **3. Reread text.** Read Prov. 8:12-21.

4. Word. What word generally describes this text?

_____

5. Phrase. Now what about that word? Expand it to a phrase:

_____

DAY 3 - SATURDAY
Thinking Day (Interpretation)

___ **1. Pray.**

___ **2. Read.** Read Prov. 7-8.

___ **3. Reread text.** Read Prov. 8:12-21.

4. Review. Write the phrase you ended up with yesterday:

_____

5. Sentence. Now expand that phrase to a sentence:

_____

6. Question. If that sentence could be turned into a question, circle the word that could be used (who, what, where, when, why, how).

Now rewrite the sentence in the form of a question:

_____

7. Answer(s). Write the many answers to your question below. These answers are all the ideas taken from the text.

_____

_____

_____

_____

DAY 4 - SUNDAY
Application Day (Application)

___ **1. Pray.**

___ **2. Read.** Read Prov. 8.

3. Combine. Try to combine the "Trunk" and the "Branches" into a complete thought here:

_____

_____

4. Apply. The BIG IDEA you just wrote is what God said. And that's what He's still saying. So now... what is He saying <u>to you</u>?

First, write some general things you learned.

_____

_____

_____

_____

_____

Next, whether you learned it from one word, the big idea, or even some random, obscure thought you had, write any other application you can think of:

_____

_____

5. Plan. Write your plan to DO something different in your life because of what you have learned.

So that I am not deceived, I plan to:

_____

_____

_____

_____

DAY 5 - MONDAY
Rereading Day

___ **1. Pray.**

___ **2. Read.** Read Prov. 7-8.

___ **3. Reread text.** Read Prov. 8:22-31.

4. Word. What word generally describes this text?

_____

5. Phrase. Now what about that word? Expand it to a phrase:

_____

Note: if you want to expand it to a sentence, go ahead!

DAY 6 - TUESDAY
Thinking Day (Interpretation)

___ **1. Pray.**

___ **2. Read.** Read Prov. 7-8.

___ **3. Reread text.** Read Prov. 8:22-31.

4. Review. Write the phrase you ended up with yesterday:

_____

5. Sentence. Now expand that phrase to a sentence:

_____

6. Question. If that sentence could be turned into a question, circle the word that could be used (who, what, where, when, why, how).

Now rewrite the sentence in the form of a question:

_____

7. Answer(s). Write the many answers to your question below. These answers are all the ideas taken from the text.

_____

_____

DAY 7 - WEDNESDAY
Application Day (Application)

___ **1. Pray.**

___ **2. Read.** Read Prov. 8.

3. Combine. Try to combine the "Trunk" and the "Branches" into a complete thought here:

_____

_____

4. Apply. The BIG IDEA you just wrote is what God said. And that's what He's still saying. So now... what is He saying <u>to you</u>?

First, write some general things you learned.

_____

_____

_____

_____

Next, whether you learned it from one word, the big idea, or even some random, obscure thought you had, write any other application you can think of:

_____

_____

5. Plan. Write your plan to DO something different in your life because of what you have learned.

So that I am not deceived, I plan to:

_____

_____

_____

Cycle 5

Proverbs 9-10

Week 1

*Initial each daily step when done.

DAY 1 - THURSDAY
Reading Day (Observation)

___ **1. Pray.** Open in prayer. Ask God's forgiveness for known sin and ask for His help in today's study.

___ **2. Background.** (see p.8 or Appendix 3 for more ideas)

_____

_____

___ **3. Read Proverbs.** Read chapters 8-12 (or more) to get the overall concept.

4. Note the text divisions. See what's coming up this week. Write the two texts you'll be studying below:

_____

DAY 2 - FRIDAY
Rereading Day

___ **1. Pray.**

___ **2. Read.** Read Prov. 9-10.

___ **3. Reread text.** Read Prov. 9:7-9.

4. Word. What word generally describes this text?

_____

5. Phrase. Now what about that word? Expand it to a phrase:

_____

Note: if you want to expand it to a sentence, go ahead!

DAY 3 - SATURDAY
Thinking Day (Interpretation)

___ **1. Pray.**

___ **2. Read.** Read Prov. 9-10.

___ **3. Reread text.** Read 9:7-9.

4. Review. Write the phrase you ended up with yesterday:

_____

5. Sentence. Now expand that phrase to a sentence:

_____

6. Question. If that sentence could be turned into a question, circle the word that could be used (who, what, where, when, why, how).

Now rewrite the sentence in the form of a question:

_____

7. Answer(s). Write the many answers to your question below. These answers are all the ideas taken from the text.

_____

_____

_____

_____

DAY 4 - SUNDAY
Application Day (Application)

___ **1. Pray.**

___ **2. Read.** Read Prov. 9.

3. Combine. Try to combine the "Trunk" and the "Branches" into a complete thought here:

_____

4. Apply. The BIG IDEA you just wrote is what God said. And that's what He's still saying. So now… what is He saying <u>to you</u>?

First, write some general things you learned.

_____

_____

_____

_____

_____

Next, whether you learned it from one word, the big idea, or even some random, obscure thought you had, write any other application you can think of:

_____

_____

5. Plan. Write your plan to DO something different in your life because of what you have learned.

So that I am not deceived, I plan to:

_____

_____

_____

DAY 5 - MONDAY
Rereading Day

___ **1. Pray.**

___ **2. Read.** Read Prov. 9-10.

___ **3. Reread text.** Read Prov. 9:13-18.

4. Word. What word generally describes this text?

_____

5. Phrase. Now what about that word? Expand it to a phrase:

_____

Note: if you want to expand it to a sentence, go ahead!

DAY 6 - TUESDAY
Thinking Day (Interpretation)

___ **1. Pray.**

___ **2. Read.** Read Prov. 9-10.

___ **3. Reread text.** Read Prov. 9:13-19.

4. Review. Write the phrase you ended up with yesterday:

_____

5. Sentence. Now expand that phrase to a sentence:

_____

6. Question. If that sentence could be turned into a question, circle the word that could be used (who, what, where, when, why, how).

Now rewrite the sentence in the form of a question:

_____

7. Answer(s). Write the many answers to your question below. These answers are all the ideas taken from the text.

_____

_____

_____

_____

_____

_____

DAY 7 - WEDNESDAY
Application Day (Application)

___ **1. Pray.**

___ **2. Read.** Read Prov. 9.

3. Combine. Try to combine the "Trunk" and the "Branches" into a complete thought here:

_____

_____

4. Apply. The BIG IDEA you just wrote is what God said. And that's what He's still saying. So now... what is He saying <u>to you</u>?

First, write some general things you learned.

_____

_____

_____

_____

_____

_____

Next, whether you learned it from one word, the big idea, or even some random, obscure thought you had, write any other application you can think of:

_____

_____

5. Plan. Write your plan to DO something different in your life because of what you have learned.

So that I am not deceived, I plan to:

_____

_____

_____

_____

WEEK 2

NOTE: The following several chapters include a collection of short Proverbs, many of them unconnected to the previous verses. Because many of the verses are self-contained truths, we will not analyze each one through the full BIBS process. Rather, each day will be a different study, culminating in a final day of application.

Initial each daily step when done.

DAY 1 - THURSDAY
Thinking Day (Interpretation)

___ **1. Pray.**

___ **2. Read.** Read Prov. 9-10.

___ **3. Reread text.** Read Prov. 10:1.

4. Interpret. What is this text about?

_____

_____

5. Reflect. What does this text mean to you? (More application coming later)

_____

_____

DAY 2 - FRIDAY
Thinking Day (Interpretation)

___ **1. Pray.**

___ **2. Read.** Read Prov. 9-10.

___ **3. Reread text.** Read Prov. 10:5.

4. Interpret. What is this text about?

_____

_____

_____

5. Reflect. What does this text mean to you? (More application coming later.)

_____

_____

🌳 DAY 3 - SATURDAY
Thinking Day (Interpretation)

___ **1. Pray.**

___ **2. Read.** Read Prov. 9-10.

___ **3. Reread text.** Read Prov. 10:9.

4. Interpret. What is this text about?

_____

_____

5. Reflect. What does this text mean to you? (More application coming later.)

_____

_____

🌳 DAY 4 - SUNDAY
Thinking Day (Interpretation)

___ **1. Pray.**

___ **2. Read.** Read Prov. 9-10.

___ **3. Reread text.** Read Prov. 10:18-21.

4. Interpret. What is this text about?

_____

_____

5. Reflect. What does this text mean to you? (More application coming later.)

_____

_____

DAY 5 - MONDAY
Thinking Day (Interpretation)

___ **1. Pray.**

___ **2. Read.** Read Prov. 9-10.

___ **3. Reread text.** Read Prov. 10:31-32.

4. Interpret. What is this text about?

_____

_____

_____

5. Reflect. What does this text mean to you? (More application coming later.)

_____

_____

DAY 6 - TUESDAY
Thinking Day (Interpretation)

___ **1. Pray.**

___ **2. Read.** Read Prov. 9-10.

___ **3. Choose text.** Reread your favorite Proverb from this chapter.

4. Background. Why did you choose this text?

_____

_____

5. Interpret. What is this text about?

_____

_____

_____

6. Reflect. What does this text mean to you? (More application coming later.)

_____

_____

DAY 7 - WEDNESDAY
Application Day (Application)

___ **1. Pray.**

___ **2. Read.** Read Prov. 10.

3. Apply. First, write some general things you learned.

_____

_____

_____

_____

_____

Next, whether you learned it from one word, the interpretation, or even some random, obscure thought you had, write any other application you can think of:

_____

_____

_____

_____

_____

_____

_____

_____

4. Plan. Write your plan to DO something different in your life because of what you have learned.

So that I am not deceived, I plan to:

_____

_____

_____

_____

_____

5. Discuss. Find someone to discuss your Bible study with. Even if it's something small that you learned, it will be a blessing to others. Remember, you're not trying to get the "right answer." You're trying to hear from God and change into His image!

CYCLE 6
Proverbs 11-12

WEEK 1

Initial each daily step when done.

 ## DAY 1 - THURSDAY
Thinking Day (Interpretation)

___ **1. Pray.**

___ **2. Read.** Read Prov. 11-12.

___ **3. Reread text.** Read Prov. 11:2.

4. Interpret. What is this text about?

_____

_____

5. Reflect. What does this text mean to you? (More application coming later)

_____

_____

 ## DAY 2 - FRIDAY
Thinking Day (Interpretation)

___ **1. Pray.**

___ **2. Read.** Read Prov. 11-12.

___ **3. Reread text.** Read Prov. 11:12-13.

4. Interpret. What is this text about?

_____

_____

5. Reflect. What does this text mean to you? (More application coming later.)

_____

_____

🌳 DAY 3 - SATURDAY
Thinking Day (Interpretation)

___ **1. Pray.**

___ **2. Read.** Read Prov. 11-12.

___ **3. Reread text.** Read Prov. 11:19.

4. Interpret. What is this text about?

_____

_____

_____

5. Reflect. What does this text mean to you? (More application coming later.)

_____

_____

🌳 DAY 4 - SUNDAY
Thinking Day (Interpretation)

___ **1. Pray.**

___ **2. Read.** Read Prov. 11-12.

___ **3. Reread text.** Read Prov. 11:21.

4. Interpret. What is this text about?

_____

_____

_____

5. Reflect. What does this text mean to you? (More application coming later.)

_____

_____

DAY 5 - MONDAY
Thinking Day (Interpretation)

___ **1. Pray.**

___ **2. Read.** Read Prov. 11-12.

___ **3. Reread text.** Read Prov. 11:24-28.

4. Interpret. What is this text about?

_____

_____

_____

5. Reflect. What does this text mean to you? (More application coming later.)

_____

_____

DAY 6 - TUESDAY
Thinking Day (Interpretation)

___ **1. Pray.**

___ **2. Read.** Read Prov. 11-12.

___ **3. Choose text.** Reread your favorite Proverb from this chapter.

4. Background. Why did you choose this text?

_____

_____

5. Interpret. What is this text about?

_____

_____

_____

6. Reflect. What does this text mean to you? (More application coming later.)

_____

_____

DAY 7 - WEDNESDAY
Application Day (Application)

___ **1. Pray.**

___ **2. Read.** Read Prov. 11.

3. Apply. First, write some general things you learned.

_____

_____

_____

_____

_____

Next, whether you learned it from one word, the interpretation, or even some random, obscure thought you had, write any other application you can think of:

_____

_____

_____

_____

_____

_____

_____

_____

_____

4. Plan. Write your plan to DO something different in your life because of what you have learned.

So that I am not deceived, I plan to:

_____

_____

_____

_____

_____

5. Discuss. Find someone to discuss your Bible study with. Even if it's something small that you learned, it will be a blessing to others. Remember, you're not trying to get the "right answer." You're trying to hear from God and change into His image!

WEEK 2

Initial each daily step when done.

 ## DAY 1 - THURSDAY
Thinking Day (Interpretation)

___ **1. Pray.**

___ **2. Read.** Read Prov. 11-12.

___ **3. Reread text.** Read Prov. 12:1.

4. Interpret. What is this text about?

_____

_____

_____

5. Reflect. What does this text mean to you? (More application coming later)

_____

_____

DAY 2 - FRIDAY
Thinking Day (Interpretation)

___ **1. Pray.**

___ **2. Read.** Read Prov. 11-12.

___ **3. Reread text.** Read Prov. 12:4.

4. Interpret. What is this text about?

_____

_____

_____

5. Reflect. What does this text mean to you? (More application coming later.)

_____

_____

DAY 3 - SATURDAY
Thinking Day (Interpretation)

___ **1. Pray.**

___ **2. Read.** Read Prov. 11-12.

___ **3. Reread text.** Read Prov. 12:12.

4. Interpret. What is this text about?

_____

_____

_____

5. Reflect. What does this text mean to you? (More application coming later.)

_____

_____

DAY 4 - SUNDAY
Thinking Day (Interpretation)

___ **1. Pray.**

___ **2. Read.** Read Prov. 11-12.

___ **3. Reread text.** Read Prov. 12:15.

4. Interpret. What is this text about?

_____

_____

_____

5. Reflect. What does this text mean to you? (More application coming later.)

_____

_____

DAY 5 - MONDAY
Thinking Day (Interpretation)

___ **1. Pray.**

___ **2. Read.** Read Prov. 11-12.

___ **3. Reread text.** Read Prov. 12:17-22.

4. Interpret. What is this text about?

_____

_____

_____

5. Reflect. What does this text mean to you? (More application coming later.)

_____

DAY 6 - TUESDAY
Thinking Day (Interpretation)

___ **1. Pray.**

___ **2. Read.** Read Prov. 11-12.

___ **3. Choose text.** Reread your favorite Proverb from this chapter.

4. Background. Why did you choose this text?

_____

_____

5. Interpret. What is this text about?

_____

_____

_____

6. Reflect. What does this text mean to you? (More application coming later.)

_____

DAY 7 - WEDNESDAY
Application Day (Application)

___ **1. Pray.**

___ **2. Read.** Read Prov. 12.

3. Apply. First, write some general things you learned.

_____

_____

_____

_____

_____

Next, whether you learned it from one word, the interpretation, or even some random, obscure thought you had, write any other application you can think of:

_____

_____

_____

_____

_____

_____

_____

_____

4. Plan. Write your plan to DO something different in your life because of what you have learned.

So that I am not deceived, I plan to:

_____

_____

_____

_____

5. Discuss. Find someone to discuss your Bible study with. Even if it's something small that you learned, it will be a blessing to others. Remember, you're not trying to get the "right answer." You're trying to hear from God and change into His image!

CYCLE 7

Proverbs 13-14

WEEK 1

Initial each daily step when done.

DAY 1 - THURSDAY
Thinking Day (Interpretation)

___ **1. Pray.**

___ **2. Read.** Read Prov. 13-14.

___ **3. Reread text.** Read Prov. 13:1.

4. Interpret. What is this text about?

_____

_____

5. Reflect. What does this text mean to you? (More application coming later)

_____

_____

DAY 2 - FRIDAY
Thinking Day (Interpretation)

___ **1. Pray.**

___ **2. Read.** Read Prov. 13-14.

___ **3. Reread text.** Read Prov. 13:10.

4. Interpret. What is this text about?

_____

_____

_____

5. Reflect. What does this text mean to you? (More application coming later.)

_____

_____

DAY 3 - SATURDAY
Thinking Day (Interpretation)

___ **1. Pray.**

___ **2. Read.** Read Prov. 13-14.

___ **3. Reread text.** Read Prov. 13:12.

4. Interpret. What is this text about?

_____

_____

_____

5. Reflect. What does this text mean to you? (More application coming later.)

_____

_____

DAY 4 - SUNDAY
Thinking Day (Interpretation)

___ **1. Pray.**

___ **2. Read.** Read Prov. 13-14.

___ **3. Reread text.** Read Prov. 13:20.

4. Interpret. What is this text about?

_____

_____

_____

5. Reflect. What does this text mean to you? (More application coming later.)

_____

_____

DAY 5 - MONDAY
Thinking Day (Interpretation)

___ **1. Pray.**

___ **2. Read.** Read Prov. 13-14.

___ **3. Reread text.** Read Prov. 13:25.

4. Interpret. What is this text about?

_____

_____

_____

5. Reflect. What does this text mean to you? (More application coming later.)

_____

_____

DAY 6 - TUESDAY
Thinking Day (Interpretation)

___ **1. Pray.**

___ **2. Read.** Read Prov. 13-14.

___ **3. Choose text.** Reread your favorite Proverb from this chapter.

4. Background. Why did you choose this text?

_____

_____

5. Interpret. What is this text about?

_____

_____

5. Reflect. What does this text mean to you? (More application coming later.)

_____

_____

DAY 7 - WEDNESDAY
Application Day (Application)

___ **1. Pray.**

___ **2. Read.** Read Prov. 13.

3. Apply. First, write some general things you learned.

_____

_____

_____

_____

_____

Next, whether you learned it from one word, the interpretation, or even some random, obscure thought you had, write any other application you can think of:

_____

_____

_____

_____

_____

_____

_____

_____

_____

4. Plan. Write your plan to DO something different in your life because of what you have learned.

So that I am not deceived, I plan to:

_____

_____

_____

_____

5. Discuss. Find someone to discuss your Bible study with. Even if it's something small that you learned, it will be a blessing to others. Remember, you're not trying to get the "right answer." You're trying to hear from God and change into His image!

WEEK 2

Initial each daily step when done.

DAY 1 - THURSDAY
Thinking Day (Interpretation)

___ **1. Pray.**

___ **2. Read.** Read Prov. 13-14.

___ **3. Reread text.** Read Prov. 14:2.

4. Interpret. What is this text about?

_____

_____

_____

5. Reflect. What does this text mean to you? (More application coming later)

_____

_____

DAY 2 - FRIDAY
Thinking Day (Interpretation)

___ **1. Pray.**

___ **2. Read.** Read Prov. 13-14.

___ **3. Reread text.** Read Prov. 14:7-9.

4. Interpret. What is this text about?

_____

_____

_____

5. Reflect. What does this text mean to you? (More application coming later.)

_____

_____

DAY 3 - SATURDAY
Thinking Day (Interpretation)

___ **1. Pray.**

___ **2. Read.** Read Prov. 13-14.

___ **3. Reread text.** Read Prov. 14:12.

4. Interpret. What is this text about?

_____

_____

_____

5. Reflect. What does this text mean to you? (More application coming later.)

_____

_____

DAY 4 - SUNDAY
Thinking Day (Interpretation)

___ **1. Pray.**

___ **2. Read.** Read Prov. 13-14.

___ **3. Reread text.** Read Prov. 14:26.

4. Interpret. What is this text about?

_____

_____

_____

5. Reflect. What does this text mean to you? (More application coming later.)

_____

_____

DAY 5 - MONDAY
Thinking Day (Interpretation)

___ **1. Pray.**

___ **2. Read.** Read Prov. 13-14.

___ **3. Reread text.** Read Prov. 14:35.

4. Interpret. What is this text about?

_____

_____

_____

5. Reflect. What does this text mean to you? (More application coming later.)

_____

_____

DAY 6 - TUESDAY
Thinking Day (Interpretation)

___ **1. Pray.**

___ **2. Read.** Read Prov. 13-14.

___ **3. Choose text.** Reread your favorite Proverb from this chapter.

4. Background. Why did you choose this text?

_____

_____

5. Interpret. What is this text about?

_____

_____

6. Reflect. What does this text mean to you? (More application coming later.)

_____

_____

DAY 7 - WEDNESDAY
Application Day (Application)

___ **1. Pray.**

___ **2. Read.** Read Prov. 14.

3. Apply. First, write some general things you learned.

_____

_____

Next, whether you learned it from one word, the interpretation, or even some random, obscure thought you had, write any other application you can think of:

_____
_____
_____
_____
_____
_____
_____
_____
_____
_____

4. Plan. Write your plan to DO something different in your life because of what you have learned.

So that I am not deceived, I plan to:

_____
_____
_____
_____
_____
_____
_____
_____
_____

5. Discuss. Find someone to discuss your Bible study with. Even if it's something small that you learned, it will be a blessing to others. Remember, you're not trying to get the "right answer." You're trying to hear from God and change into His image!

CYCLE 8

Proverbs 15-16

WEEK 1

Initial each daily step when done.

 ## DAY 1 - THURSDAY
Thinking Day (Interpretation)

___ **1. Pray.**

___ **2. Read.** Read Prov. 15-16.

___ **3. Reread text.** Read Prov. 15:1-4.

4. Interpret. What is this text about?

_____

_____

_____

5. Reflect. What does this text mean to you? (More application coming later)

_____

_____

DAY 2 - FRIDAY
Thinking Day (Interpretation)

___ **1. Pray.**

___ **2. Read.** Read Prov. 15-16.

___ **3. Reread text.** Read Prov. 15:8.

4. Interpret. What is this text about?

_____

_____

5. Reflect. What does this text mean to you? (More application coming later.)

_____

_____

DAY 3 - SATURDAY
Thinking Day (Interpretation)

___ **1. Pray.**

___ **2. Read.** Read Prov. 15-16.

___ **3. Reread text.** Read Prov. 15:10.

4. Interpret. What is this text about?

_____

_____

_____

5. Reflect. What does this text mean to you? (More application coming later.)

_____

_____

DAY 4 - SUNDAY
Thinking Day (Interpretation)

___ **1. Pray.**

___ **2. Read.** Read Prov. 15-16.

___ **3. Reread text.** Read Prov. 15:13.

4. Interpret. What is this text about?

_____

_____

_____

5. Reflect. What does this text mean to you? (More application coming later.)

_____

DAY 5 - MONDAY
Thinking Day (Interpretation)

___ **1. Pray.**

___ **2. Read.** Read Prov. 15-16.

___ **3. Reread text.** Read Prov. 15:32-33.

4. Interpret. What is this text about?

_____

_____

_____

5. Reflect. What does this text mean to you? (More application coming later.)

_____

_____

DAY 6 - TUESDAY
Thinking Day (Interpretation)

___ **1. Pray.**

___ **2. Read.** Read Prov. 15-16.

___ **3. Choose text.** Reread your favorite Proverb from this chapter.

4. Background. Why did you choose this text?

_____

_____

5. Interpret. What is this text about?

_____

_____

_____

6. Reflect. What does this text mean to you? (More application coming later.)

_____

_____

DAY 7 - WEDNESDAY
Application Day (Application)

___ **1. Pray.**

___ **2. Read.** Read Prov. 15.

3. Apply. First, write some general things you learned.

_____

_____

_____

_____

_____

Next, whether you learned it from one word, the interpretation, or even some random, obscure thought you had, write any other application you can think of:

_____

_____

_____

_____

_____

_____

_____

_____

4. Plan. Write your plan to DO something different in your life because of what you have learned.

So that I am not deceived, I plan to:

_____

_____

_____

_____

5. Discuss. Find someone to discuss your Bible study with. Even if it's something small that you learned, it will be a blessing to others. Remember, you're not trying to get the "right answer." You're trying to hear from God and change into His image!

WEEK 2

Initial each daily step when done.

 ## DAY 1 - THURSDAY
Thinking Day (Interpretation)

___ **1. Pray.**

___ **2. Read.** Read Prov. 15-16.

___ **3. Reread text.** Read Prov. 16:9.

4. Interpret. What is this text about?

_____

_____

_____

5. Reflect. What does this text mean to you? (More application coming later)

_____

_____

DAY 2 - FRIDAY
Thinking Day (Interpretation)

___ **1. Pray.**

___ **2. Read.** Read Prov. 15-16.

___ **3. Reread text.** Read Prov. 16:16.

4. Interpret. What is this text about?

_____

_____

_____

5. Reflect. What does this text mean to you? (More application coming later.)

_____

_____

DAY 3 - SATURDAY
Thinking Day (Interpretation)

___ **1. Pray.**

___ **2. Read.** Read Prov. 15-16.

___ **3. Reread text.** Read Prov. 16:18.

4. Interpret. What is this text about?

_____

_____

_____

5. Reflect. What does this text mean to you? (More application coming later.)

_____

_____

DAY 4 - SUNDAY
Thinking Day (Interpretation)

___ **1. Pray.**

___ **2. Read.** Read Prov. 15-16.

___ **3. Reread text.** Read Prov. 16:27-30.

4. Interpret. What is this text about?

_____

_____

_____

5. Reflect. What does this text mean to you? (More application coming later.)

_____

_____

DAY 5 - MONDAY
Thinking Day (Interpretation)

___ **1. Pray.**

___ **2. Read.** Read Prov. 15-16.

___ **3. Reread text.** Read Prov. 16:32.

4. Interpret. What is this text about?

_____

_____

_____

5. Reflect. What does this text mean to you? (More application coming later.)

_____

_____

DAY 6 - TUESDAY
Thinking Day (Interpretation)

___ **1. Pray.**

___ **2. Read.** Read Prov. 15-16.

___ **3. Choose text.** Reread your favorite Proverb from this chapter.

4. Background. Why did you choose this text?

_____

_____

5. Interpret. What is this text about?

_____

_____

_____

6. Reflect. What does this text mean to you? (More application coming later.)

_____

_____

DAY 7 - WEDNESDAY
Application Day (Application)

___ **1. Pray.**

___ **2. Read.** Read Prov. 16.

3. Apply. First, write some general things you learned.

_____

_____

_____

_____

_____

Next, whether you learned it from one word, the interpretation, or even some random, obscure thought you had, write any other application you can think of:

_____

_____

_____

_____

_____

_____

_____

_____

_____

4. Plan. Write your plan to DO something different in your life because of what you have learned.

So that I am not deceived, I plan to:

_____

_____

_____

_____

_____

_____

_____

5. Discuss. Find someone to discuss your Bible study with. Even if it's something small that you learned, it will be a blessing to others. Remember, you're not trying to get the "right answer." You're trying to hear from God and change into His image!

CYCLE 9

Proverbs 17-18

WEEK 1

Initial each daily step when done.

DAY 1 - THURSDAY
Thinking Day (Interpretation)

___ **1. Pray.**

___ **2. Read.** Read Prov. 17-18.

___ **3. Reread text.** Read Prov. 17:3.

4. Interpret. What is this text about?

_____

_____

5. Reflect. What does this text mean to you? (More application coming later)

_____

_____

DAY 2 - FRIDAY
Thinking Day (Interpretation)

___ **1. Pray.**

___ **2. Read.** Read Prov. 17-18.

___ **3. Reread text.** Read Prov. 17:15.

4. Interpret. What is this text about?

_____

_____

_____

5. Reflect. What does this text mean to you? (More application coming later.)

_____

_____

🌳 DAY 3 - SATURDAY
Thinking Day (Interpretation)

___ **1. Pray.**

___ **2. Read.** Read Prov. 17-18.

___ **3. Reread text.** Read Prov. 17:22.

4. Interpret. What is this text about?

_____

_____

_____

5. Reflect. What does this text mean to you? (More application coming later.)

_____

_____

🌳 DAY 4 - SUNDAY
Thinking Day (Interpretation)

___ **1. Pray.**

___ **2. Read.** Read Prov. 17-18.

___ **3. Reread text.** Read Prov. 17:25.

4. Interpret. What is this text about?

_____

_____

_____

5. Reflect. What does this text mean to you? (More application coming later.)

_____

DAY 5 - MONDAY
Thinking Day (Interpretation)

___ **1. Pray.**

___ **2. Read.** Read Prov. 17-18.

___ **3. Reread text.** Read Prov. 17:27-28.

4. Interpret. What is this text about?

_____

_____

_____

5. Reflect. What does this text mean to you? (More application coming later.)

_____

_____

DAY 6 - TUESDAY
Thinking Day (Interpretation)

___ **1. Pray.**

___ **2. Read.** Read Prov. 17-18.

___ **3. Choose text.** Reread your favorite Proverb from this chapter.

4. Background. Why did you choose this text?

_____

_____

5. Interpret. What is this text about?

_____

_____

_____

6. Reflect. What does this text mean to you? (More application coming later.)

_____

_____

DAY 7 - WEDNESDAY
Application Day (Application)

___ **1. Pray.**

___ **2. Read.** Read Prov. 17.

3. Apply. First, write some general things you learned.

_____

_____

_____

_____

_____

_____

Next, whether you learned it from one word, the interpretation, or even some random, obscure thought you had, write any other application you can think of:

_____

_____

_____

_____

_____

4. Plan. Write your plan to DO something different in your life because of what you have learned.

So that I am not deceived, I plan to:

_____

_____

_____

_____

_____

5. Discuss. Find someone to discuss your Bible study with. Even if it's something small that you learned, it will be a blessing to others. Remember, you're not trying to get the "right answer." You're trying to hear from God and change into His image!

WEEK 2

Initial each daily step when done.

DAY 1 - THURSDAY
Thinking Day (Interpretation)

___ **1. Pray.**

___ **2. Read.** Read Prov. 17-18.

___ **3. Reread text.** Read Prov. 18:1-2.

4. Interpret. What is this text about?

_____

_____

_____

5. Reflect. What does this text mean to you? (More application coming later)

_____

_____

DAY 2 - FRIDAY
Thinking Day (Interpretation)

___ **1. Pray.**

___ **2. Read.** Read Prov. 17-18.

___ **3. Reread text.** Read Prov. 18:9.

4. Interpret. What is this text about?

_____

_____

_____

5. Reflect. What does this text mean to you? (More application coming later.)

_____

DAY 3 - SATURDAY
Thinking Day (Interpretation)

___ **1. Pray.**

___ **2. Read.** Read Prov. 17-18.

___ **3. Reread text.** Read Prov. 18:13.

4. Interpret. What is this text about?

_____

_____

_____

5. Reflect. What does this text mean to you? (More application coming later.)

_____

_____

DAY 4 - SUNDAY
Thinking Day (Interpretation)

___ **1. Pray.**

___ **2. Read.** Read Prov. 17-18.

___ **3. Reread text.** Read Prov. 18:22.

4. Interpret. What is this text about?

_____

_____

_____

5. Reflect. What does this text mean to you? (More application coming later.)

_____

_____

DAY 5 - MONDAY
Thinking Day (Interpretation)

___ **1. Pray.**

___ **2. Read.** Read Prov. 17-18.

___ **3. Reread text.** Read Prov. 18:24.

4. Interpret. What is this text about?

_____

_____

_____

5. Reflect. What does this text mean to you? (More application coming later.)

_____

_____

DAY 6 - TUESDAY
Thinking Day (Interpretation)

___ **1. Pray.**

___ **2. Read.** Read Prov. 17-18.

___ **3. Choose text.** Reread your favorite Proverb from this chapter.

4. Background. Why did you choose this text?

_____

_____

5. Interpret. What is this text about?

_____

_____

_____

6. Reflect. What does this text mean to you? (More application coming later.)

_____

_____

DAY 7 - WEDNESDAY
Application Day (Application)

___ **1. Pray.**

___ **2. Read.** Read Prov. 18.

3. Apply. First, write some general things you learned.

_____

_____

_____

_____

_____

Next, whether you learned it from one word, the interpretation, or even some random, obscure thought you had, write any other application you can think of:

_____

_____

_____

_____

_____

_____

_____

_____

4. Plan. Write your plan to DO something different in your life because of what you have learned.

So that I am not deceived, I plan to:

_____

_____

_____

_____

5. Discuss. Find someone to discuss your Bible study with. Even if it's something small that you learned, it will be a blessing to others. Remember, you're not trying to get the "right answer." You're trying to hear from God and change into His image!

CYCLE 10

WEEK 1

Initial each daily step when done.

DAY 1 - THURSDAY
Thinking Day (Interpretation)

___ **1. Pray.**

___ **2. Read.** Read Prov. 19-20.

___ **3. Reread text.** Read Prov. 19:11.

4. Interpret. What is this text about?

_____

_____

_____

5. Reflect. What does this text mean to you? (More application coming later)

_____

_____

DAY 2 - FRIDAY
Thinking Day (Interpretation)

___ **1. Pray.**

___ **2. Read.** Read Prov. 19-20.

___ **3. Reread text.** Read Prov. 19:13.

4. Interpret. What is this text about?

_____

_____

5. Reflect. What does this text mean to you? (More application coming later.)

_____

_____

🌳 DAY 3 - SATURDAY
Thinking Day (Interpretation)

___ **1. Pray.**

___ **2. Read.** Read Prov. 19-20.

___ **3. Reread text.** Read Prov. 19:15.

4. Interpret. What is this text about?

_____

_____

_____

5. Reflect. What does this text mean to you? (More application coming later.)

_____

_____

🌳 DAY 4 - SUNDAY
Thinking Day (Interpretation)

___ **1. Pray.**

___ **2. Read.** Read Prov. 19-20.

___ **3. Reread text.** Read Prov. 19:21.

4. Interpret. What is this text about?

_____

_____

_____

5. Reflect. What does this text mean to you? (More application coming later.)

_____

DAY 5 - MONDAY
Thinking Day (Interpretation)

___ **1. Pray.**

___ **2. Read.** Read Prov. 19-20.

___ **3. Reread text.** Read Prov. 19:27.

4. Interpret. What is this text about?

_____

_____

_____

5. Reflect. What does this text mean to you? (More application coming later.)

_____

_____

DAY 6 - TUESDAY
Thinking Day (Interpretation)

___ **1. Pray.**

___ **2. Read.** Read Prov. 19-20.

___ **3. Choose text.** Reread your favorite Proverb from this chapter.

4. Background. Why did you choose this text?

_____

_____

5. Interpret. What is this text about?

_____

_____

_____

5. Reflect. What does this text mean to you? (More application coming later.)

_____

_____

 # DAY 7 - WEDNESDAY
Application Day (Application)

___ **1. Pray.**

___ **2. Read.** Read Prov. 19.

3. Apply. First, write some general things you learned.

_____

_____

_____

_____

_____

Next, whether you learned it from one word, the interpretation, or even some random, obscure thought you had, write any other application you can think of:

_____

_____

_____

_____

_____

_____

_____

_____

_____

4. Plan. Write your plan to DO something different in your life because of what you have learned.

So that I am not deceived, I plan to:

_____

_____

_____

_____

5. Discuss. Find someone to discuss your Bible study with. Even if it's something small that you learned, it will be a blessing to others. Remember, you're not trying to get the "right answer." You're trying to hear from God and change into His image!

WEEK 2

Initial each daily step when done.

DAY 1 - THURSDAY
Thinking Day (Interpretation)

___ **1. Pray.**

___ **2. Read.** Read Prov. 19-20.

___ **3. Reread text.** Read Prov. 20:1.

4. Interpret. What is this text about?

_____

_____

_____

5. Reflect. What does this text mean to you? (More application coming later)

_____

_____

DAY 2 - FRIDAY
Thinking Day (Interpretation)

___ **1. Pray.**

___ **2. Read.** Read Prov. 19-20.

___ **3. Reread text.** Read Prov. 20:3.

4. Interpret. What is this text about?

_____

_____

_____

5. Reflect. What does this text mean to you? (More application coming later.)

_____

_____

DAY 3 - SATURDAY
Thinking Day (Interpretation)

___ **1. Pray.**

___ **2. Read.** Read Prov. 19-20.

___ **3. Reread text.** Read Prov. 20:6.

4. Interpret. What is this text about?

_____

_____

_____

5. Reflect. What does this text mean to you? (More application coming later.)

_____

_____

DAY 4 - SUNDAY
Thinking Day (Interpretation)

___ **1. Pray.**

___ **2. Read.** Read Prov. 19-20.

___ **3. Reread text.** Read Prov. 20:13.

4. Interpret. What is this text about?

_____

_____

_____

5. Reflect. What does this text mean to you? (More application coming later.)

_____

_____

DAY 5 - MONDAY
Thinking Day (Interpretation)

___ **1. Pray.**

___ **2. Read.** Read Prov. 19-20.

___ **3. Reread text.** Read Prov. 20:29.

4. Interpret. What is this text about?

_____

_____

_____

5. Reflect. What does this text mean to you? (More application coming later.)

_____

_____

DAY 6 - TUESDAY
Thinking Day (Interpretation)

___ **1. Pray.**

___ **2. Read.** Read Prov. 19-20.

___ **3. Choose text.** Reread your favorite Proverb from this chapter.

4. Background. Why did you choose this text?

_____

_____

5. Interpret. What is this text about?

_____

_____

_____

6. Reflect. What does this text mean to you? (More application coming later.)

_____

_____

DAY 7 - WEDNESDAY
Application Day (Application)

___ **1. Pray.**

___ **2. Read.** Read Prov. 20.

3. Apply. First, write some general things you learned.

_____

_____

_____

_____

_____

Next, whether you learned it from one word, the interpretation, or even some random, obscure thought you had, write any other application you can think of:

_____

_____

_____

_____

_____

_____

_____

_____

4. Plan. Write your plan to DO something different in your life because of what you have learned.

So that I am not deceived, I plan to:

_____

_____

_____

_____

_____

5. Discuss. Find someone to discuss your Bible study with. Even if it's something small that you learned, it will be a blessing to others. Remember, you're not trying to get the "right answer." You're trying to hear from God and change into His image!

CYCLE 11

Proverbs 21-22

WEEK 1

Initial each daily step when done.

DAY 1 - THURSDAY
Thinking Day (Interpretation)

___ **1. Pray.**

___ **2. Read.** Read Prov. 21-22.

___ **3. Reread text.** Read Prov. 21:6.

4. Interpret. What is this text about?

_____

_____

_____

5. Reflect. What does this text mean to you? (More application coming later)

_____

_____

DAY 2 - FRIDAY
Thinking Day (Interpretation)

___ **1. Pray.**

___ **2. Read.** Read Prov. 21-22.

___ **3. Reread text.** Read Prov. 21:9.

4. Interpret. What is this text about?

_____

_____

5. Reflect. What does this text mean to you? (More application coming later.)

_____

_____

🌳 DAY 3 - SATURDAY
Thinking Day (Interpretation)

___ **1. Pray.**

___ **2. Read.** Read Prov. 21-22.

___ **3. Reread text.** Read Prov. 21:12.

4. Interpret. What is this text about?

_____

_____

_____

5. Reflect. What does this text mean to you? (More application coming later.)

_____

_____

🌳 DAY 4 - SUNDAY
Thinking Day (Interpretation)

___ **1. Pray.**

___ **2. Read.** Read Prov. 21-22.

___ **3. Reread text.** Read Prov. 21:17.

4. Interpret. What is this text about?

_____

_____

_____

5. Reflect. What does this text mean to you? (More application coming later.)

_____

DAY 5 - MONDAY
Thinking Day (Interpretation)

___ **1. Pray.**

___ **2. Read.** Read Prov. 21-22.

___ **3. Reread text.** Read Prov. 21:30.

4. Interpret. What is this text about?

_____

_____

_____

5. Reflect. What does this text mean to you? (More application coming later.)

_____

_____

DAY 6 - TUESDAY
Thinking Day (Interpretation)

___ **1. Pray.**

___ **2. Read.** Read Prov. 21-22.

___ **3. Choose text.** Reread your favorite Proverb from this chapter.

4. Background. Why did you choose this text?

_____

_____

5. Interpret. What is this text about?

_____

_____

_____

5. Reflect. What does this text mean to you? (More application coming later.)

_____

_____

DAY 7 - WEDNESDAY
Application Day (Application)

___ **1. Pray.**

___ **2. Read.** Read Prov. 21.

3. Apply. First, write some general things you learned.

_____

_____

_____

_____

_____

Next, whether you learned it from one word, the interpretation, or even some random, obscure thought you had, write any other application you can think of:

_____

_____

_____

_____

_____

_____

_____

_____

4. Plan. Write your plan to DO something different in your life because of what you have learned.

So that I am not deceived, I plan to:

_____

_____

_____

_____

5. Discuss. Find someone to discuss your Bible study with. Even if it's something small that you learned, it will be a blessing to others. Remember, you're not trying to get the "right answer." You're trying to hear from God and change into His image!

WEEK 2

Initial each daily step when done.

DAY 1 - THURSDAY
Thinking Day (Interpretation)

___ **1. Pray.**

___ **2. Read.** Read Prov. 21-22.

___ **3. Reread text.** Read Prov. 22:1.

4. Interpret. What is this text about?

_____

_____

_____

5. Reflect. What does this text mean to you? (More application coming later)

_____

_____

DAY 2 - FRIDAY
Thinking Day (Interpretation)

___ **1. Pray.**

___ **2. Read.** Read Prov. 21-22.

___ **3. Reread text.** Read Prov. 22:4.

4. Interpret. What is this text about?

_____

_____

_____

5. Reflect. What does this text mean to you? (More application coming later.)

_____

_____

DAY 3 - SATURDAY
Thinking Day (Interpretation)

___ **1. Pray.**

___ **2. Read.** Read Prov. 21-22.

___ **3. Reread text.** Read Prov. 22:15.

4. Interpret. What is this text about?

_____

_____

_____

5. Reflect. What does this text mean to you? (More application coming later.)

_____

_____

DAY 4 - SUNDAY
Thinking Day (Interpretation)

___ **1. Pray.**

___ **2. Read.** Read Prov. 21-22.

___ **3. Reread text.** Read Prov. 22:17-21.

4. Interpret. What is this text about?

_____

_____

_____

5. Reflect. What does this text mean to you? (More application coming later.)

_____

_____

DAY 5 - MONDAY
Thinking Day (Interpretation)

___ **1. Pray.**

___ **2. Read.** Read Prov. 21-22.

___ **3. Reread text.** Read Prov. 22:24-25.

4. Interpret. What is this text about?

_____

_____

_____

5. Reflect. What does this text mean to you? (More application coming later.)

_____

_____

DAY 6 - TUESDAY
Thinking Day (Interpretation)

___ **1. Pray.**

___ **2. Read.** Read Prov. 21-22.

___ **3. Choose text.** Reread your favorite Proverb from this chapter.

4. Background. Why did you choose this text?

_____

_____

5. Interpret. What is this text about?

_____

_____

_____

6. Reflect. What does this text mean to you? (More application coming later.)

_____

_____

DAY 7 - WEDNESDAY
Application Day (Application)

___ **1. Pray.**

___ **2. Read.** Read Prov. 22.

3. Apply. First, write some general things you learned.

_____

_____

_____

_____

_____

Next, whether you learned it from one word, the interpretation, or even some random, obscure thought you had, write any other application you can think of:

_____

_____

_____

_____

_____

_____

_____

_____

_____

_____

4. Plan. Write your plan to DO something different in your life because of what you have learned.

So that I am not deceived, I plan to:

_____

_____

_____

_____

5. Discuss. Find someone to discuss your Bible study with. Even if it's something small that you learned, it will be a blessing to others. Remember, you're not trying to get the "right answer." You're trying to hear from God and change into His image!

CYCLE 12

Proverbs 23-24

WEEK 1

Initial each daily step when done.

 ## DAY 1 - THURSDAY
Thinking Day (Interpretation)

___ **1. Pray.**

___ **2. Read.** Read Prov. 23-24.

___ **3. Reread text.** Read Prov. 23:1-8.

4. Interpret. What is this text about?

_____

_____

5. Reflect. What does this text mean to you? (More application coming later)

_____

_____

DAY 2 - FRIDAY
Thinking Day (Interpretation)

___ **1. Pray.**

___ **2. Read.** Read Prov. 23-24.

___ **3. Reread text.** Read Prov. 23:12.

4. Interpret. What is this text about?

_____

_____

_____

5. Reflect. What does this text mean to you? (More application coming later.)

_____

_____

DAY 3 - SATURDAY
Thinking Day (Interpretation)

___ **1. Pray.**

___ **2. Read.** Read Prov. 23-24.

___ **3. Reread text.** Read Prov. 23:17-18.

4. Interpret. What is this text about?

_____

_____

_____

5. Reflect. What does this text mean to you? (More application coming later.)

_____

_____

DAY 4 - SUNDAY
Thinking Day (Interpretation)

___ **1. Pray.**

___ **2. Read.** Read Prov. 23-24.

___ **3. Reread text.** Read Prov. 23:20-21.

4. Interpret. What is this text about?

_____

_____

_____

5. Reflect. What does this text mean to you? (More application coming later.)

_____

DAY 5 - MONDAY
Thinking Day (Interpretation)

___ **1. Pray.**

___ **2. Read.** Read Prov. 23-24.

___ **3. Reread text.** Read Prov. 23:29-35.

4. Interpret. What is this text about?

_____

_____

_____

5. Reflect. What does this text mean to you? (More application coming later.)

_____

_____

DAY 6 - TUESDAY
Thinking Day (Interpretation)

___ **1. Pray.**

___ **2. Read.** Read Prov. 23-24.

___ **3. Choose text.** Reread your favorite Proverb from this chapter.

4. Background. Why did you choose this text?

_____

_____

5. Interpret. What is this text about?

_____

_____

_____

6. Reflect. What does this text mean to you? (More application coming later.)

_____

_____

DAY 7 - WEDNESDAY
Application Day (Application)

___ **1. Pray.**

___ **2. Read.** Read Prov. 23.

3. Apply. First, write some general things you learned.

_____

_____

_____

_____

_____

_____

Next, whether you learned it from one word, the interpretation, or even some random, obscure thought you had, write any other application you can think of:

_____

_____

_____

_____

_____

_____

4. Plan. Write your plan to DO something different in your life because of what you have learned.

So that I am not deceived, I plan to:

_____

_____

_____

_____

_____

_____

5. Discuss. Find someone to discuss your Bible study with. Even if it's something small that you learned, it will be a blessing to others. Remember, you're not trying to get the "right answer." You're trying to hear from God and change into His image!

WEEK 2

Initial each daily step when done.

DAY 1 - THURSDAY
Thinking Day (Interpretation)

___ **1. Pray.**

___ **2. Read.** Read Prov. 23-24.

___ **3. Reread text.** Read Prov. 24:1-2.

4. Interpret. What is this text about?

_____

_____

_____

5. Reflect. What does this text mean to you? (More application coming later)

_____

_____

DAY 2 - FRIDAY
Thinking Day (Interpretation)

___ **1. Pray.**

___ **2. Read.** Read Prov. 23-24.

___ **3. Reread text.** Read Prov. 24:10.

4. Interpret. What is this text about?

_____

_____

_____

5. Reflect. What does this text mean to you? (More application coming later.)

_____

DAY 3 - SATURDAY
Thinking Day (Interpretation)

___ **1. Pray.**

___ **2. Read.** Read Prov. 23-24.

___ **3. Reread text.** Read Prov. 24:16.

4. Interpret. What is this text about?

_____

_____

_____

5. Reflect. What does this text mean to you? (More application coming later.)

_____

_____

DAY 4 - SUNDAY
Thinking Day (Interpretation)

___ **1. Pray.**

___ **2. Read.** Read Prov. 23-24.

___ **3. Reread text.** Read Prov. 24:19-20.

4. Interpret. What is this text about?

_____

_____

_____

5. Reflect. What does this text mean to you? (More application coming later.)

_____

_____

DAY 5 - MONDAY
Thinking Day (Interpretation)

___ **1. Pray.**

___ **2. Read.** Read Prov. 23-24.

___ **3. Reread text.** Read Prov. 24:30-34.

4. Interpret. What is this text about?

_____

_____

_____

5. Reflect. What does this text mean to you? (More application coming later.)

_____

_____

DAY 6 - TUESDAY
Thinking Day (Interpretation)

___ **1. Pray.**

___ **2. Read.** Read Prov. 23-24.

___ **3. Choose text.** Reread your favorite Proverb from this chapter.

4. Background. Why did you choose this text?

_____

_____

5. Interpret. What is this text about?

_____

_____

_____

6. Reflect. What does this text mean to you? (More application coming later.)

_____

_____

# DAY 7 - WEDNESDAY
Application Day (Application)

___ **1. Pray.**

___ **2. Read.** Read Prov. 24.

3. Apply. First, write some general things you learned.

_____

_____

_____

_____

_____

Next, whether you learned it from one word, the interpretation, or even some random, obscure thought you had, write any other application you can think of:

_____

_____

_____

_____

_____

_____

_____

_____

4. Plan. Write your plan to DO something different in your life because of what you have learned.

So that I am not deceived, I plan to:

_____

_____

_____

_____

5. Discuss. Find someone to discuss your Bible study with. Even if it's something small that you learned, it will be a blessing to others. Remember, you're not trying to get the "right answer." You're trying to hear from God and change into His image!

CYCLE 13

Proverbs 25-26

WEEK 1

Initial each daily step when done.

 ## DAY 1 - THURSDAY
Thinking Day (Interpretation)

___ **1. Pray.**

___ **2. Read.** Read Prov. 25-26.

___ **3. Reread text.** Read Prov. 25:11.

4. Interpret. What is this text about?

_____

_____

_____

5. Reflect. What does this text mean to you? (More application coming later)

_____

_____

DAY 2 - FRIDAY
Thinking Day (Interpretation)

___ **1. Pray.**

___ **2. Read.** Read Prov. 25-26.

___ **3. Reread text.** Read Prov. 25:13.

4. Interpret. What is this text about?

_____

_____

5. Reflect. What does this text mean to you? (More application coming later.)

_____

_____

🌳 DAY 3 - SATURDAY
Thinking Day (Interpretation)

___ **1. Pray.**

___ **2. Read.** Read Prov. 25-26.

___ **3. Reread text.** Read Prov. 25:19.

4. Interpret. What is this text about?

_____

_____

_____

5. Reflect. What does this text mean to you? (More application coming later.)

_____

_____

🌳 DAY 4 - SUNDAY
Thinking Day (Interpretation)

___ **1. Pray.**

___ **2. Read.** Read Prov. 25-26.

___ **3. Reread text.** Read Prov. 25:21-22.

4. Interpret. What is this text about?

_____

_____

_____

5. Reflect. What does this text mean to you? (More application coming later.)

_____

DAY 5 - MONDAY
Thinking Day (Interpretation)

___ **1. Pray.**

___ **2. Read.** Read Prov. 25-26.

___ **3. Reread text.** Read Prov. 25:24.

4. Interpret. What is this text about?

_____

_____

_____

5. Reflect. What does this text mean to you? (More application coming later.)

_____

_____

DAY 6 - TUESDAY
Thinking Day (Interpretation)

___ **1. Pray.**

___ **2. Read.** Read Prov. 25-26.

___ **3. Choose text.** Reread your favorite Proverb from this chapter.

4. Background. Why did you choose this text?

_____

_____

5. Interpret. What is this text about?

_____

_____

_____

5. Reflect. What does this text mean to you? (More application coming later.)

_____

_____

DAY 7 - WEDNESDAY
Application Day (Application)

___ **1. Pray.**

___ **2. Read.** Read Prov. 25.

3. Apply. First, write some general things you learned.

_____

_____

_____

_____

_____

Next, whether you learned it from one word, the interpretation, or even some random, obscure thought you had, write any other application you can think of:

_____

_____

_____

_____

_____

_____

_____

_____

4. Plan. Write your plan to DO something different in your life because of what you have learned.

So that I am not deceived, I plan to:

_____

_____

_____

_____

5. Discuss. Find someone to discuss your Bible study with. Even if it's something small that you learned, it will be a blessing to others. Remember, you're not trying to get the "right answer." You're trying to hear from God and change into His image!

WEEK 2

Initial each daily step when done.

DAY 1 - THURSDAY
Thinking Day (Interpretation)

___ **1. Pray.**

___ **2. Read.** Read Prov. 25-26.

___ **3. Reread text.** Read Prov. 26:4-5.

4. Interpret. What is this text about?

_____

_____

_____

5. Reflect. What does this text mean to you? (More application coming later)

_____

_____

DAY 2 - FRIDAY
Thinking Day (Interpretation)

___ **1. Pray.**

___ **2. Read.** Read Prov. 25-26.

___ **3. Reread text.** Read Prov. 26:11.

4. Interpret. What is this text about?

_____

_____

_____

5. Reflect. What does this text mean to you? (More application coming later.)

_____

_____

DAY 3 - SATURDAY
Thinking Day (Interpretation)

___ **1. Pray.**

___ **2. Read.** Read Prov. 25-26.

___ **3. Reread text.** Read Prov. 26:13-16.

4. Interpret. What is this text about?

_____

_____

_____

5. Reflect. What does this text mean to you? (More application coming later.)

_____

_____

DAY 4 - SUNDAY
Thinking Day (Interpretation)

___ **1. Pray.**

___ **2. Read.** Read Prov. 25-26.

___ **3. Reread text.** Read Prov. 26:20-21.

4. Interpret. What is this text about?

_____

_____

_____

5. Reflect. What does this text mean to you? (More application coming later.)

_____

_____

DAY 5 - MONDAY
Thinking Day (Interpretation)

___ **1. Pray.**

___ **2. Read.** Read Prov. 25-26.

___ **3. Reread text.** Read Prov. 26:27-28.

4. Interpret. What is this text about?

_____

_____

_____

5. Reflect. What does this text mean to you? (More application coming later.)

_____

_____

DAY 6 - TUESDAY
Thinking Day (Interpretation)

___ **1. Pray.**

___ **2. Read.** Read Prov. 25-26.

___ **3. Choose text.** Reread your favorite Proverb from this chapter.

4. Background. Why did you choose this text?

_____

_____

5. Interpret. What is this text about?

_____

_____

_____

6. Reflect. What does this text mean to you? (More application coming later.)

_____

_____

DAY 7 - WEDNESDAY
Application Day (Application)

___ **1. Pray.**

___ **2. Read.** Read Prov. 26.

3. Apply. First, write some general things you learned.

_____

_____

_____

_____

_____

Next, whether you learned it from one word, the interpretation, or even some random, obscure thought you had, write any other application you can think of:

_____

_____

_____

_____

_____

_____

_____

4. Plan. Write your plan to DO something different in your life because of what you have learned.

So that I am not deceived, I plan to:

_____

_____

_____

_____

_____

5. Discuss. Find someone to discuss your Bible study with. Even if it's something small that you learned, it will be a blessing to others. Remember, you're not trying to get the "right answer." You're trying to hear from God and change into His image!

Cycle 14

Proverbs 27-28

Week 1

Initial each daily step when done.

 ## DAY 1 - THURSDAY
Thinking Day (Interpretation)

___ **1. Pray.**

___ **2. Read.** Read Prov. 27-28.

___ **3. Reread text.** Read Prov. 27:1.

4. Interpret. What is this text about?

_____

_____

_____

5. Reflect. What does this text mean to you? (More application coming later)

_____

_____

DAY 2 - FRIDAY
Thinking Day (Interpretation)

___ **1. Pray.**

___ **2. Read.** Read Prov. 27-28.

___ **3. Reread text.** Read Prov. 27:5-6.

4. Interpret. What is this text about?

_____

_____

5. Reflect. What does this text mean to you? (More application coming later.)

_____

_____

DAY 3 - SATURDAY
Thinking Day (Interpretation)

___ **1. Pray.**

___ **2. Read.** Read Prov. 27-28.

___ **3. Reread text.** Read Prov. 27:9.

4. Interpret. What is this text about?

_____

_____

_____

5. Reflect. What does this text mean to you? (More application coming later.)

_____

_____

DAY 4 - SUNDAY
Thinking Day (Interpretation)

___ **1. Pray.**

___ **2. Read.** Read Prov. 27-28.

___ **3. Reread text.** Read Prov. 27:12.

4. Interpret. What is this text about?

_____

_____

_____

5. Reflect. What does this text mean to you? (More application coming later.)

_____

DAY 5 - MONDAY
Thinking Day (Interpretation)

___ **1. Pray.**

___ **2. Read.** Read Prov. 27-28.

___ **3. Reread text.** Read Prov. 27:17-22.

4. Interpret. What is this text about?

_____

_____

_____

5. Reflect. What does this text mean to you? (More application coming later.)

_____

_____

DAY 6 - TUESDAY
Thinking Day (Interpretation)

___ **1. Pray.**

___ **2. Read.** Read Prov. 27-28.

___ **3. Choose text.** Reread your favorite Proverb from this chapter.

4. Background. Why did you choose this text?

_____

_____

5. Interpret. What is this text about?

_____

_____

_____

5. Reflect. What does this text mean to you? (More application coming later.)

_____

_____

DAY 7 - WEDNESDAY
Application Day (Application)

___ **1. Pray.**

___ **2. Read.** Read Prov. 27.

3. Apply. First, write some general things you learned.

_____

_____

_____

_____

_____

Next, whether you learned it from one word, the interpretation, or even some random, obscure thought you had, write any other application you can think of:

_____

_____

_____

_____

_____

_____

_____

_____

4. Plan. Write your plan to DO something different in your life because of what you have learned.

So that I am not deceived, I plan to:

_____

_____

_____

_____

5. Discuss. Find someone to discuss your Bible study with. Even if it's something small that you learned, it will be a blessing to others. Remember, you're not trying to get the "right answer." You're trying to hear from God and change into His image!

WEEK 2

Initial each daily step when done.

DAY 1 - THURSDAY
Thinking Day (Interpretation)

___ **1. Pray.**

___ **2. Read.** Read Prov. 27-28.

___ **3. Reread text.** Read Prov. 28:1.

4. Interpret. What is this text about?

_____

_____

_____

5. Reflect. What does this text mean to you? (More application coming later)

_____

_____

DAY 2 - FRIDAY
Thinking Day (Interpretation)

___ **1. Pray.**

___ **2. Read.** Read Prov. 27-28.

___ **3. Reread text.** Read Prov. 28:8.

4. Interpret. What is this text about?

_____

_____

_____

5. Reflect. What does this text mean to you? (More application coming later.)

_____

_____

DAY 3 - SATURDAY
Thinking Day (Interpretation)

___ **1. Pray.**

___ **2. Read.** Read Prov. 27-28.

___ **3. Reread text.** Read Prov. 28:13.

4. Interpret. What is this text about?

_____

_____

_____

5. Reflect. What does this text mean to you? (More application coming later.)

_____

_____

DAY 4 - SUNDAY
Thinking Day (Interpretation)

___ **1. Pray.**

___ **2. Read.** Read Prov. 27-28.

___ **3. Reread text.** Read Prov. 28:18.

4. Interpret. What is this text about?

_____

_____

_____

5. Reflect. What does this text mean to you? (More application coming later.)

_____

_____

DAY 5 - MONDAY
Thinking Day (Interpretation)

___ **1. Pray.**

___ **2. Read.** Read Prov. 27-28.

___ **3. Reread text.** Read Prov. 28:20.

4. Interpret. What is this text about?

_____

_____

_____

5. Reflect. What does this text mean to you? (More application coming later.)

_____

_____

DAY 6 - TUESDAY
Thinking Day (Interpretation)

___ **1. Pray.**

___ **2. Read.** Read Prov. 27-28.

___ **3. Choose text.** Reread your favorite Proverb from this chapter.

4. Background. Why did you choose this text?

_____

_____

5. Interpret. What is this text about?

_____

_____

_____

6. Reflect. What does this text mean to you? (More application coming later.)

_____

_____

DAY 7 - WEDNESDAY
Application Day (Application)

___ **1. Pray.**

___ **2. Read.** Read Prov. 28.

3. Apply. First, write some general things you learned.

_____

_____

_____

_____

_____

Next, whether you learned it from one word, the interpretation, or even some random, obscure thought you had, write any other application you can think of:

_____

_____

_____

_____

_____

_____

_____

_____

4. Plan. Write your plan to DO something different in your life because of what you have learned.

So that I am not deceived, I plan to:

_____

_____

_____

_____

5. Discuss. Find someone to discuss your Bible study with. Even if it's something small that you learned, it will be a blessing to others. Remember, you're not trying to get the "right answer." You're trying to hear from God and change into His image!

CYCLE 15

Proverbs 29-31

WEEK 1

Initial each daily step when done.

 ## DAY 1 - THURSDAY
Thinking Day (Interpretation)

___ **1. Pray.**

___ **2. Read.** Read Prov. 29-31.

___ **3. Reread text.** Read Prov. 29:1, 11, 20, 23, and 25.

4. Interpret each text individually. What is this text about?

V1_____

_____

V11_____

_____

V20_____

_____

V23_____

_____

V25_____

_____

5. Reflect. What do these texts mean to you?

_____

_____

_____

_____

DAY 2 - FRIDAY
Rereading Day

___ **1. Pray.**

___ **2. Read.** Read Prov. 29-31.

___ **3. Reread text.** Read Prov. 30:2-4.

4. Word. What word generally describes this text?

_____

5. Phrase. Now what about that word? Expand it to a phrase:

_____

Note: if you want to expand it to a sentence, go ahead!

DAY 3 - SATURDAY
Thinking Day (Interpretation)

___ **1. Pray.**

___ **2. Read.** Read Prov. 30-31.

___ **3. Reread text.** Read Prov. 30:2-4.

4. Review. Write the phrase you ended up with yesterday:

_____

5. Sentence. Now expand that phrase to a sentence:

_____

6. Question. If that sentence could be turned into a question, circle the word that could be used (who, what, where, when, why, how).

Now rewrite the sentence in the form of a question:

_____

7. Answer(s). Write the many answers to your question below. These answers are all the ideas taken from the text.

_____

_____

_____

_____

DAY 4 - SUNDAY
Application Day (Application)

___ **1. Pray.**

___ **2. Read.** Read Prov. 30.

3. Combine. Try to combine the "Trunk" and the "Branches" into a complete thought here:

_____

_____

4. Apply. The BIG IDEA you just wrote is what God said. And that's what He's still saying. So now... what is He saying <u>to you</u>?

First, write some general things you learned.

_____

_____

_____

_____

Next, whether you learned it from one word, the big idea, or even some random, obscure thought you had, write any other application you can think of:

_____

_____

5. Plan. Write your plan to DO something different in your life because of what you have learned.

So that I am not deceived, I plan to:

_____

_____

_____

DAY 5 - MONDAY
Rereading Day

___ **1. Pray.**

___ **2. Read.** Read Prov. 29-31.

___ **3. Reread text.** Read Prov. 30:15-17.

4. Word. What word generally describes this text?

_____

5. Phrase. Now what about that word? Expand it to a phrase:

_____

Note: if you want to expand it to a sentence, go ahead!

🌳 DAY 6 - TUESDAY
🍸 Thinking Day (Interpretation)

___ **1. Pray.**

___ **2. Read.** Read Prov. 30-31.

___ **3. Reread text.** Read Prov. 30:15-17.

4. Review. Write the phrase you ended up with yesterday:

_____

5. Sentence. Now expand that phrase to a sentence:

_____

6. Question. If that sentence could be turned into a question, circle the word that could be used (who, what, where, when, why, how).

Now rewrite the sentence in the form of a question:

_____

7. Answer(s). Write the many answers to your question below. These answers are all the ideas taken from the text.

_____

_____

_____

_____

_____

_____

DAY 7 - WEDNESDAY
Application Day (Application)

___ **1. Pray.**

___ **2. Read.** Read Prov. 30.

3. Combine. Try to combine the "Trunk" and the "Branches" into a complete thought here:

_____

_____

4. Apply. The BIG IDEA you just wrote is what God said. And that's what He's still saying. So now... what is He saying <u>to you</u>?

First, write some general things you learned.

_____

_____

_____

_____

_____

Next, whether you learned it from one word, the big idea, or even some random, obscure thought you had, write any other application you can think of:

_____

_____

5. Plan. Write your plan to DO something different in your life because of what you have learned.

So that I am not deceived, I plan to:

_____

_____

_____

_____

WEEK 2

*Initial each daily step when done.

DAY 1 - THURSDAY
Rereading Day (much OBS. has been done)

___ **1. Pray.**

___ **2. Read.** Read Prov. 29-31.

___ **3. Reread text.** Read Prov. 30:24-28.

4. Word. What word generally describes this text?

_____

5. Phrase. Now what about that word? Expand it to a phrase:

_____

6. Sentence. Expand that phrase to a sentence:

_____

DAY 2 - FRIDAY
Thinking Day (Interpretation)

___ **1. Pray.**

___ **2. Read.** Read Prov. 30-31.

___ **3. Reread text.** Read Prov. 30:24-28.

4. Review. Write the sentence you ended up with yesterday:

_____

5. Question. If that sentence could be turned into a question, circle the word that could be used (who, what, where, when, why, how).

Now rewrite the sentence in the form of a question:

_____

6. Answer(s). Write the many answers to your question below. These answers are all the ideas taken from the text.

_____

_____

_____

_____

_____

7. Apply. Tomorrow will not be application, so write a few thoughts of your own below:

_____

_____

_____

_____

DAY 3 - SATURDAY
Rereading Day (Interpretation)

___ **1. Pray.**

___ **2. Read.** Read Prov. 29-31.

___ **3. Reread text.** Read Prov. 31:1-5.

4. Word. What word generally describes this text?

_____

5. Phrase. Now what about that word? Expand it to a phrase:

_____

6. Sentence. Expand that phrase to a sentence:

_____

DAY 4 - SUNDAY
Thinking Day (Interpretation)

___ **1. Pray.**

___ **2. Read.** Read Prov. 31.

___ **3. Reread text.** Read Prov. 31:1-5.

4. Review. Write the sentence you ended up with yesterday:

_____

5. Question. If that sentence could be turned into a question, circle the word that could be used (who, what, where, when, why, how).

Now rewrite the sentence in the form of a question:

_____

6. Answer(s). Write the many answers to your question below. These answers are all the ideas taken from the text.

_____

_____

_____

_____

7. Apply. Tomorrow will not be application, so write a few thoughts of your own below:

_____

_____

DAY 5 - MONDAY
Rereading Day (Interpretation)

___ **1. Pray.**

___ **2. Read.** Read Prov. 30-31.

___ **3. Reread text.** Read Prov. 31:10-31

4. Word. What word generally describes this text?

_____

5. Phrase. Now what about that word? Expand it to a phrase:

_____

6. Sentence. Expand that phrase to a sentence:

_____

_____

DAY 6 - TUESDAY
Thinking Day (Interpretation)

___ **1. Pray.**

___ **2. Read.** Read Prov. 30-31.

___ **3. Reread text.** Read Prov. 31:10-31.

4. Review. Write the sentence you ended up with yesterday:

_____

5. Question. If that sentence could be turned into a question, circle the word that could be used (who, what, where, when, why, how).

Now rewrite the sentence in the form of a question:

_____

6. Answer(s). Write the many answers to your question below. These answers are all the ideas taken from the text.

_____

_____

_____

_____

_____

_____

_____

DAY 7 - WEDNESDAY
Application Day (Application)

___ **1. Pray.**

___ **2. Read.** Read Prov. 2.

3. Combine. Write the three "trees" you found (from days 2, 4, 6):

_____

_____

_____

_____

_____

4. Apply. The BIG IDEAS you just wrote were what God said. And that's what He's still saying. So now... what is He saying to you?

First, write some general things you learned.

_____
_____
_____
_____
_____
_____

Next, whether you learned it from one word, the big idea, or even some random, obscure thought you had, write any other application you can think of:

_____
_____
_____
_____
_____
_____
_____
_____
_____

5. Plan. Write your plan to DO something different in your life because of what you have learned.

So that I am not deceived, I plan to:

_____
_____
_____
_____
_____
_____
_____

6. Discuss. Find someone to discuss your Bible study with. Even if it's something small that you learned, it will be a blessing to others. Remember, you're not trying to get the "right answer." You're trying to hear from God and change into His image!

APPENDIX 1 - Sources for Ideas

The ideas for the structure, layout and format of this devotional book are derived from several different sources, although the exact structure is unique as what we are calling our BIBS model. Although our church does not necessarily agree with every aspect of each of these authors' teachings, ideas were taken from the following:

- ***My Biography of God*, by Sam Brock.** *My Biography of God* is a daily devotional set up in a one-week format. Each week the reader studies a certain passage every day and answers questions from the text that lead him to conclusions about God. The conclusions are written in various formats throughout the book, including attributes about God, names of God and more. *My Biography of God* is produced by *Iron Sharpeneth Iron*--the publication ministry of Ironwood Christian Camp.

- ***Living by the Book*, by Howard Hendricks.** *Living by the Book* is a book divided into clear sections emphasizing various Bible study techniques. The main idea borrowed from this book was that Bible study should be done in a sequence of observation, interpretation and application.

- ***How to Read the Bible for All Its Worth*, by Gordon Fee and Douglas Stewart.** *How to...* is an instructional book on interpreting various biblical genres.

- ***Biblical Preaching*, by Haddon Robinson.** *Biblical Preaching* is an instructional book on how to study the Bible in order to present a single concept (big idea) through preaching. Many examples in the BIBS explanations and appendices are taken from *Biblical Preaching*. Further examples included are the concepts about the subject and complement.

- ***Invitation to Biblical Preaching*, by Don Sunukjian.** *Invitation to Biblical Preaching* is an instructional book on how to study the Bible in order to present a single concept (big idea) through preaching. The main wording borrowed for the BIBS format are the questions: "What is God saying?" (big idea) and "What is God saying *to us*?" (application)

APPENDIX 2 - More on Biblical Genres

Article Source[1]

The Basic Genres:

History or **Narrative:** There are stories and the epics and include Genesis, Exodus, Numbers, Joshua, Judges, Ruth, 1 and 2 Samuel, 1 and 2 Kings, 1 and 2 Chronicles, Ezra, Nehemiah, Esther, Jonah, and Acts.

Law: These are the instructions and precepts of God given to us through Moses, such as Leviticus and Deuteronomy.

Wisdom: These are the literature of maxims and sayings such as Job, Proverbs, and Ecclesiastes.

Poetry: These are the prose and rhymes such as Psalms, Song of Solomon, and Lamentations.

Prophecy: These include both major and minor prophets such as Isaiah, Jeremiah, Ezekiel, Daniel, Hosea, Joel, Amos, Obadiah, Micah, Nahum, Habakkuk, Zephaniah, Haggai, Zechariah, and Malachi.

Apocalyptic: These are combinations of narrative and prose written in vivid imagery and poetic phrases such as Daniel and most of Revelation.*

Parable: These are the sayings of Jesus that are narrative and instructional, contained in the Gospels.

Epistle: These are the letters written to a specific audience that are practical for us today such as Romans, Corinthians, Galatians, Ephesians, Philippians, Colossians, Thessalonians, Timothy, Titus, Philemon, Hebrews, James, Peter, John, and the first three chapters of Revelation.

Romance: These are narrative, written also as love stories, such as Ruth and Song of Solomon.

---

1   http://sites.silaspartners.com/intothy-word

Then, ask how the type of *genre* (type of literature) shows you the significance and implication of the general overview?

How does the type of *genre* contribute to possible meanings of specific words and then the point of the passage?

Biblical Genres Include:

Law: This contains the instructions and precepts of Moses, such as Leviticus and Deuteronomy. Law is "God's law", and is the expression of His sovereign will and character. The writings of Moses contain a lot of Law. God provided the Jews with many laws (619 or so). These laws defined the proper relationship with God, to one another, and with the world (the alien), as well as for worshiping God, governing the people, priestly duties, what to eat and not eat, how to build the temple, proper behavior, manners, and social interaction, etc. The Ten Commandments are often known as "The Law;" so are Exodus, Leviticus, Numbers, and Deuteronomy. In the New Testament, the "Sermon on the Mount" is considered law and the fulfillment of the law, and Paul's calls to the church are law in their literature form.

Most Christians have a distorted view of the law and think it does not apply to us. Jesus repeated and affirmed the Ten Commandments and the Law of Moses. The law points to our depravity and need for a Savior. Without the law, there would be no relationship to God or need for Christ to save us. Christ fulfills the law and thus we are not bound to its curse, but we must acknowledge its role in our lives as the pointer to the Cross and the mirror to our soul.

History or **Narrative:** These are the stories and the epics, and include: Genesis, Exodus, Numbers, Joshua, Judges, Ruth, 1 and 2 Samuel, 1 and 2 Kings, 1 and 2 Chronicles, Ezra, Nehemiah, Esther, Jonah, and Acts. Almost every Old Testament book contains history. Some books of the Bible are grouped together and commonly referred to as the "History" (Joshua, Kings, and Chronicles); these books tell us the history of the Jewish people from the time of the Judges through the Persian Empire. In the New Testament, Acts contains some of the history of the early church, and the Gospels also have history; Jesus' life is told as history. Even the Epistles have history as they chronicle events. There is also anther sub-category of narrative called "Romance;" this is narrative written also as a love story such as Ruth and Song of Solomon.

Wisdom: This is the literature of maxims and sayings, including Job, Proverbs, and Ecclesiastes. Wisdom Literature focuses on questions about the meaning of life (Job, Ecclesiastes) and on practical living and common sense (Proverbs and some Psalms). This literature contrasts our faulty human wisdom to God's reasoning perfection. Thus, when we live for our own will and not His, we will experience grief and frustration, not because God is vengeful and angry, but because we led ourselves that way out of our pride and arrogance. This literature warns us of our evil nature and desires.

Poetry: These are the prose and rhyme books such as Psalms, Song of Solomon, and Lamentations. Poetry is found mostly in the Old Testament and is similar to modern poetry. Since the poetical books were originally written in Hebrew, the English translation appears different from what we tend to think of as poetry, with its rhymes and rhythmic phrases.* Poetry that we are used to is usually based on parallelisms, rhythm, or various types of sound mixing, as is our music. Hebrew poetry is based on a tempo of stanzas and phrases re-told differently called "synonymous parallelism", conveying the same ideas and meaning in contrasting or similar ways. Some called "synthetic parallelism," also have extra ideas and words inserted. "Antithetic parallelism" is mostly contrasting stanzas, and is very predominant in Proverbs. Some Bible books are all poetry (Psalms, Song of Songs, and Lamentations), and some books only have a few verses such as in Luke.

Gospel: This word means the "good news" that we received through salvation by the work and life of God's Son, Jesus Christ. When the Gospels were first written in the first century, it was a brand new form of literature. The four Gospels (Mark, Matthew, Luke, and John) contain a bit of all the literary types with the primary purpose of expressing faith in Christ and what He has done on our behalf. In these works, the stories are not necessarily in chronological or sequential order, except for Luke. In this type of literature, we find what is called a "Parable." These are the sayings of Jesus that are narrative and instructional, contained in the Gospels. Each of the gospels presents the teachings, ministry, death, and resurrection of Jesus in a distinctive way, but not contradictory, and for a specific audience. Matthew was written to Jews, and Luke to Greeks, both with different ways of reasoning and thinking. Think of the Gospels like the facets of a diamond, giving more depth and meaning.

Parables: These are the sayings of Jesus told in a short story or illustration form that are narrative and instructional; they teach a truth, and are contained in the Gospels. Usually, these are from everyday life examples that may have taken place or may not. At times, such as in the Parable of the Sower, Jesus was possibly pointing to it as He taught. These had a deeper purpose than the face value of the illustration, thus it took some thinking and a desire to learn in order to understand them. Perhaps, He used them to keep people of impiety and without intent of faith from bothering Him; or, perhaps He wanted to challenge the skeptics and people who were unresponsive.

Epistle: This refers to the 21 letters in the New Testament written to a specific audience that are also practical for us today such as Romans, Corinthians, Galatians, Ephesians, Philippians, Colossians, Thessalonians, Timothy, Titus, Philemon, Hebrews, James, Peter, John, and the first three chapters of Revelation. Epistles are the personal letters from the Apostles to their churches. These letters are both different and similar to the letters of their time. Most challenge the congregation to wake up out of their selfish ways and to concentrate on Christ in specific ways and clarifications. They begin with the names of the writer and the recipient, then a greeting, a reason for the letter, and then the central message or body of the letter; there is usually a closing, just like most letters today.

The epistles deal with concerns and false teachings that needed immediate correction. Some epistles were written in response to questions from the church, or for clarification for another letter, such as II Corinthians. The teachings of the epistles applied to both to the church they were written to, and also to Christians today. However, we need to understand the cultural and historical situation to better understand what is going on, so we do not misunderstand what is being said.

Prophecy means past, present, and future, not just the future. This includes major and minor prophets—Isaiah, Jeremiah, Ezekiel, Daniel, Hosea, Joel, Amos, Obadiah, Micah, Nahum, Habakkuk, Zephaniah, Haggai, Zechariah, and Malachi. Prophecy is the type of literature that is often associated with predicting the future. However, it also contains God's words of "get with it or else." There are two main types. One is "predictive," as in foretelling an event, and the other is "didactic," challenging others to line up morally or to teach a truth. Thus, prophecy also exposes sin and calls for repentance and obedience. It shows how God's law can be applied to specific problems and situations, such as the repeated warnings to the Jews before their captivity. This is found in the Old Testament books of Isaiah through Malachi, the section of the Bible labeled "Prophecy" by both Jews and Christians. There are over 2,000 specific predictions that have already come to pass, hundreds of years after the author's death!

In the New Testament, prophecy is mainly found in Matthew 24-25, the Thessalonians* and the book of Revelation. Prophecy has both an immediate call to a given situation, such as the "seven churches of Revelation", and a predated future to come to pass. That is, it is two fold—a past and a future, both applying to the present. Some predictions are already fulfilled, such as the birth, life, death, and resurrection of Jesus Christ and some have yet to come to pass such as sections of Daniel, 2 Peter, Revelation, and the return of Christ.

Apocalyptic: These are combinations of narrative and prose written in vivid imagery and poetic phrases that are intended for a purpose such as Daniel and most of Revelation. Apocalyptic writing is a more specific form of prophecy, and is a type of literature that warns us of future events. Apocalyptic writing is found in Isaiah, Daniel, Ezekiel, Zechariah, and Revelation.*

* edits made

APPENDIX 3 - Examples

EXAMPLE 1 - PSALM 117

1. O praise the Lord, all ye nations: praise him, all ye people.

2. For his merciful kindness is great toward us: and the truth of the Lord endureth for ever. Praise ye the Lord.

OBSERVATION

We know very little about the Psalm itself, but because it's a Psalm we understand that it is probably to God or about God.

INTERPRETATION

Read and reread the text. Done. Didn't take long.

Flag words. I understand all the words, but looking up certain words adds depth to my understanding.

V2 - Great - Prevail. Have strength. Mighty. Confirm, give strength.

V2 - Endureth for ever. Everlasting. Eternal. Unending future.

Word. Praise

Phrase. Praise the Lord

Sentence. We should praise the Lord.

Question Word. Why?

Question. Why should we praise the Lord?

Answers: 1) His merciful kindness and 2) His truth endures.

Big Idea. We should praise the Lord because His mercy is great toward us and His truth endures forever.

APPLICATION

First, God is merciful to me. Why does He choose to be merciful? Why does He have to be merciful? What is He merciful toward? Why would He be called merciful? If He's merciful, that must mean that He is holding back some kind of wrath or punishment.

I certainly deserve a lot of punishment for my sin. I know my own heart; my own lusts. I know what I'm like when no one is around. And... wow... God shows mercy to me every day. What an amazing God! He is so longsuffering with my sin, and He allows me the chance to repent and forsake my sin. God, thank you for showing mercy.

Second, His kindness. God not only does NOT give me punishment when I deserve it, but he DOES give me things that I do not deserve.

Thank you, God, for being so merciful to me. Thank you, on top of that, for being kind and giving me so much. I don't deserve my healthy body, but You are kind enough to give it to me. I have a great family, parents who love me, a loving church to attend, friends who want to help me, I live in America and I'm spoiled rotten with all the conveniences you give me. Thank you, God.

Third, You're not only merciful and kind, but those qualities are GREAT toward me! Why would you offer me mercy even once? And why in the world do You KEEP being merciful and kind even when you know my heart?! You have heaped on the blessings over and over, and I never really thank you properly for it.

The second "branch" was about your truth. I was allowed to read Your very words to me. I can know that there's something true in my life because Your Word has never been proven wrong. It is Truth. And it's still around. And no matter how many people have tried and will try to attack it, it still endures. It's forever! It's eternal. No other book is like that. Thank you, God, that I can know Your Truth!

All this, God... Your merciful kindness that is GREAT toward me... and Your wonderful Truth that you allow me to know and study. How can I keep silent about you?! You're SO good to me! And I too often fail You. Forgive me, God. But more than that, I PRAISE you! Praise God for being SO good to me! Thank you God! I want to serve You more and MORE every day!

MY PLAN: So that I am not deceived, I plan to attend church this Sunday morning and night and REALLY take part in the praise portion of our services. I'm going to sing loud, concentrate on the words, have a heart of gratitude and let is show on my face this Sunday. Hopefully everyone will be able to tell this praise is finally real with me.

Example 2 - Finding the Big-Idea

The following examples are taken from Haddon Robinson's Biblical Preaching *(pp.44-45). They are examples from Habakkuk. Mr. Robinson describes the "trunk" as the subject and the "branches" as the complement. These examples skip the first few steps of the BIBS approach and, after much study, arrive at the "question" step of the BIBS format.*

Look at how the process works with the poetry in an Old Testament book. The small diary of Habakkuk consists of a series of conversations that the prophet had with God. In the opening chapter, Habakkuk is upset with God for not punishing evil in the nation of Judah and in the broader world. We must first state the ideas that make up the argument the prophet had with God.

Habakkuk opens with a complaint in 1:2-4. Stated as a subject and complement, this is the idea:

Subject: What is Habakkuk's lament about the injustice he sees in Judah?

Complement: He wonders why God, who is righteous, doesn't judge the nation for its sin.

Idea: Habakkuk laments that his righteous God does not punish sin in Judah.

God replies to the prophet in 1:5-7. God's answer can also be stated as a subject and complement:

Subject: How will God bring judgment on Judah?

Complement: God will use the wicked Babylonians to punish His people.

Idea: God will use the wicked Babylonians to punish His people.

Note that both of these paragraphs (1:2-11) can now be joined in a larger subject and complement:

Subject: How will God punish the evil and injustice rampant in His people, Judah?

Complement: God will use the wicked Babylonians as His whipping stick.

Idea: God will judge the evil in His own people, Judah, through an invasion by the wicked Babylonians.

That leads us, then, to the third paragraph in the passage found in 1:12-2:1:

Subject: How could a righteous God use the evil and godless Babylonian to punish a more righteous nation like Judah?

Complement: God will also punish the Babylonians at an appointed time.

Idea: Even though God will use the wicked Babylonians to punish Judah, He will also judge the Babylonians for their sin.

Made in the USA
Monee, IL
19 August 2024

64167187R00083